CAMPAIGN 83

CORUNNA 1809

SIR JOHN MOORE'S FIGHTING RETREAT

SERIES EDITOR: LEE JOHNSON

CAMPAIGN 83

CORUNNA 1809

SIR JOHN MOORE'S FIGHTING RETREAT

WRITTEN BY
PHILIP HAYTHORNTHWAITE

BATTLESCENE PLATES BY
CHRISTA HOOK

First published in Great Britain in 2001 by Osprey Publishing, Elms Court, Chapel Way, Botley, Oxford OX2 9LP United Kingdom
Email: info@ospreypublishing.com

ISBN 1 85532 968 9

Editor: Lee Johnson
Design: The Black Spot

Colour bird's-eye view illustrations by The Black Spot
Cartography by The Map Studio
Battlescene artwork by Christa Hook
Index by Alan Rutter
Originated by Magnet Harlequin, Uxbridge, UK
Printed in China through World Print Ltd.

01 02 03 04 05   10 9 8 7 6 5 4 3 2 1

For a catalogue of all books published by Osprey Military and Aviation please write to:

The Marketing Manager, Osprey Publishing Ltd., P.O. Box 140, Wellingborough, Northants NN8 4ZA United Kingdom
Email: info@ospreydirect.co.uk

The Marketing Manager, Osprey Direct USA, c/o Motorbooks International, P.O. Box 1, Osceola, WI 54020-0001, USA

Buy online at www.ospreypublishing.com

Author's Note

The correct spelling of the place-name is La Coruña, but the version used most commonly in English-language sources is 'Corunna'. It is also the spelling used, from an early date, for the battle-honour granted to those British regiments which were present, although it is worth remarking that on the belt-plate adopted after the grant of the honour in 1812, the 50th Foot used the correct Spanish spelling 'Coruña'.

Acknowledgements

The author extends his thanks to John Cox, Thomas E. DeVoe, and especially to Ian Fletcher of Ian Fletcher Battlefield Tours of Rochester, Kent, for both advice and the supply of photographs.

Editor's Note

Full details are given in the footnotes for those titles referred to which do not appear in the bibliography.

Artist's Note

KEY TO MILITARY SYMBOLS

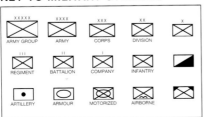

CONTENTS

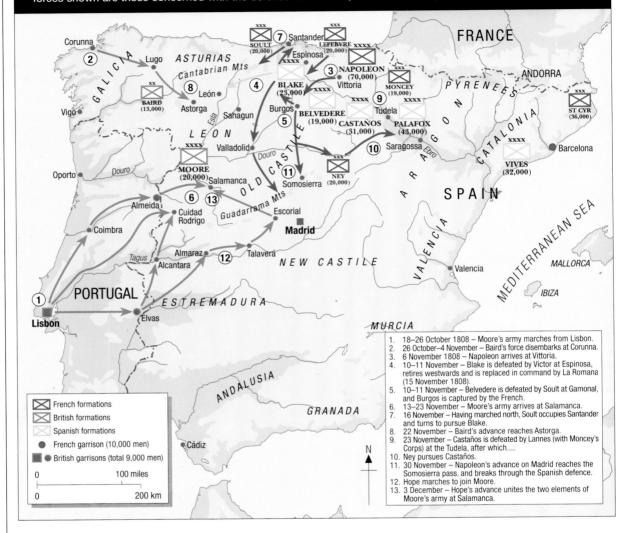

THE CAMPAIGN IN SPAIN, OCTOBER–DECEMBER 1808

The French centre under Napoleon included the corps of Victor, Bessières (later Soult, which was sent west against Blake), Ney (sent east against Castanos), the Imperial Guard and reserve cavalry. The only Spanish forces shown are those concerned with the defence of the Ebro, and in Catalonia; others existed elsewhere.

FRANCE

ANDORRA

PYRENEES

GALICIA

Corunna

②

Lugo

ASTURIAS

Cantabrian Mts

SOULT (20,000)

⑦ Santander

Espinosa

LEFEBVRE (20,000)

③ NAPOLEON (70,000)

Vittoria

MONCEY (19,000)

ST CYR (36,000)

Vigó

BAIRD (13,000)

⑧ León

Astorga

④

BLAKE (23,000)

Burgos

BELVEDERE (19,000)

CASTAÑOS (31,000)

Tudela

⑨

PALAFOX (43,000)

Saragossa

ARAGON

CATALONIA

Barcelona

LEON

Sahagun

Esla

⑤

VIVES (32,000)

Oporto

Douro

Valladolid

MOORE (20,000)

Salamanca

OLD CASTILE

Douro

⑪

Somosierra

NEY (20,000)

Ebro

SPAIN

⑩

⑥ ⑬

Almeida

Cuidad Rodrigo

Guadarrama Mts

Escorial

Madrid

VALENCIA

MEDITERRANEAN SEA

MALLORCA

Coimbra

Tagus

Almaraz

⑫ Talavera

NEW CASTILE

Valencia

IBIZA

Alcantara

①

PORTUGAL

ESTREMADURA

Lisbon

Elvas

MURCIA

ANDALUSIA

GRANADA

Cádiz

N

Legend:

- ⊠ French formations
- ⊠ British formations
- ⊠ Spanish formations
- ● French garrison (10,000 men)
- ■● British garrisons (total 9,000 men)

0 — 100 miles
0 — 200 km

1. 18–26 October 1808 – Moore's army marches from Lisbon.
2. 26 October–4 November – Baird's force disembarks at Corunna.
3. 6 November 1808 – Napoleon arrives at Vittoria.
4. 10–11 November – Blake is defeated by Victor at Espinosa, retires westwards and is replaced in command by La Romana (15 November 1808).
5. 10–11 November – Belvedere is defeated by Soult at Gamonal, and Burgos is captured by the French.
6. 13–23 November – Moore's army arrives at Salamanca.
7. 16 November – Having marched north, Soult occupies Santander and turns to pursue Blake.
8. 22 November – Baird's advance reaches Astorga.
9. 23 November – Castaños is defeated by Lannes (with Moncey's Corps) at the Tudela, after which....
10. Ney pursues Castaños.
11. 30 November – Napoleon's advance on Madrid reaches the Somosierra pass, and breaks through the Spanish defence.
12. Hope marches to join Moore.
13. 3 December – Hope's advance unites the two elements of Moore's army at Salamanca.

ORIGINS OF THE CAMPAIGN

Robert Stewart, Viscount Castlereagh, later 2nd Marquess of Londonderry (1769–1822), Secretary for War, a supporter of the British expedition to the Peninsula. (Engraving by T.W. Harland after Sir Thomas Lawrence)

Sir John Moore (1761–1809): an early portrait.

The Corunna campaign arose from the determination of the British government to continue its opposition to Napoleon by supporting the inhabitants of the Iberian peninsula in their attempt to resist French occupation. The first revolts in Spain convinced the British ministry that aid should be sent, for as the Foreign Secretary, George Canning, declared in the House of Commons on 15 June 1808, any opponent of France became an ally of Great Britain, and that involvement in the Peninsula was a matter of British national interest, for 'no interest can be so purely British as Spanish success'.

Initially an expedition was sent to Portugal, where rebellion was threatening the tenuous hold on Lisbon maintained by the French army of General Andoche Junot. Command of the expedition was entrusted in the first instance to Sir Arthur Wellesley, a general with a successful record in India and a 'friend' of the ministry, of which he had himself been a part. His initial force was to have a substantial reinforcement under Sir John Moore, who had recently returned from an abortive expedition to the Baltic. Wellesley's senior, Moore enjoyed a high reputation in the army and had a charismatic personality, but was regarded as a political opponent of the ministry; indeed, Moore has been described as 'the Whig general par excellence'.[1] It is perhaps worth remarking, however, that his employment by a Tory ministry demonstrates that political favouritism was not a dominant factor in the determination of such appointments. Nevertheless, while Moore's abilities were probably too obvious to be ignored, his relationship with Lord Castlereagh, Secretary of State for War, was initially somewhat strained, and elements in the government seem to have doubted the wisdom of appointing him. Thus it was decided to place over his head (and thus over that of Wellesley) another general, Sir Hew Dalrymple, then commanding at Gibraltar. It is likely that Dalrymple was intended to be a temporary appointment only, until he might be replaced by the Earl of Chatham (brother of the late Prime Minister, William Pitt), or until Wellesley distinguished himself sufficiently to be given control of the enlarged expedition. Perhaps to prevent Moore from taking command should any mishap befall Dalrymple, Sir Harry Burrard was appointed as the latter's official second in command.

Such decisions must have been severe blows to both Moore and Wellesley, but the nature of both men led them to place public service before personal dignity, and due to their mutual respect the two could have worked well together – as Wellington said he told Moore, 'you are the man, and I shall with great willingness act under you'.[2]

In the event that never occurred. Wellesley's expedition landed and defeated Junot's French army at Rolica (17 August 1808) and Vimeiro (21 August), although the arrival of the over-cautious Burrard prevented exploitation of the success. Upon Dalrymple's arrival in chief command, Junot was able to negotiate the Convention of Cintra, by which French forces were evacuated by sea from Portugal – with baggage and loot intact – instead of being compelled to surrender. Although it did secure for Britain a Portuguese base without further fighting, the convention was greeted with outrage in Britain. The three British generals were recalled for an inquiry, from which only Wellesley emerged with his reputation unscathed – he had acquiesced to the convention only with the greatest reluctance. With the removal of these three, however, Moore was left in command of the British forces in Portugal, from 6 October 1808.

By this time, Napoleon's plans for the peninsula were going awry. Although his brother Joseph had been installed as king of Spain in place of the legitimate royal family, he was accepted by only a small minority of the Spanish population, insurrection was widespread, and several Spanish armies were in the field to oppose him. On 19 July 1808 the French cause had suffered a severe blow with the surrender of General Pierre Dupont's army to the Spanish forces of Xavier Castaños at Baylen, and the loss of Portugal compounded the situation. Napoleon's exasperation is evident from his correspondence with Joseph, who following Baylen had abandoned his capital, Madrid: 'Dupont has dishonoured our flag. What incapacity, what cowardice! … All that goes on in Spain is deplorable. The army seems to be commanded, not by generals or soldiers, but by postmasters'.[3]

Napoleon's solution, as might have been expected, was not only to increase dramatically the number of French troops in Spain, but to take command in person. After ensuring that there would be no immediate distractions from central Europe arising from his absence – confirming his alliance with Russia in a conference at Erfurt and making veiled threats against Austria – Napoleon was free to transfer veteran divisions to Spain, and on 3 November arrived at Bayonne in person.

Sir John Moore in the uniform of a lieutenant-general. (Engraving by Charles Turner after Sir Thomas Lawrence)

1 Anderson p.55
2 Stanhope, Earl, *Notes on Conversations with the Duke of Wellington*, London 1888, p.244
3 Napoleon, Vol.I pp.343, 346

OPPOSING COMMANDERS

THE FRENCH

Joseph Bonaparte, King of Spain (1768–1844), whose installation as king by Napoleon was a primary cause of the Peninsular War. (Engraving by L. Rados after J.B. Bosio)

Although he did not command in person in any of the actions against Moore, **Napoleon Bonaparte**'s presence in Spain can hardly be over-emphasised. In the winter of 1808 he was probably near the peak of his military powers, his most recent campaigns having resulted in the rapid and overwhelming defeat of Prussia in 1806, and the succeeding victories over Russia at Eylau and Friedland. The importance of Napoleon's presence in the theatre of war extended beyond his own battlefield talents. He was able to supervise the army's administration and remedy many of its faults, and more significantly to impose an overall strategy with a clarity of direction which had been lacking, and which could not have been achieved from a greater distance. In the later Peninsular campaigns, French operations suffered from the virtual independence of the various armies, and from the mutual dislikes and jealousies among the commanders, which seriously impaired collaboration. Without Napoleon's presence in 1808 it is possible these factors might have occurred as they did in succeeding years. In Napoleon's next campaign, the war against Austria in 1809, he was to suffer the first serious check to his military career, which might be taken as a sign that his abilities had begun to wane; but although his time in Spain was relatively short, it resulted in an immense improvement in French fortunes.

For his campaign in Spain, Napoleon organised the French forces into eight (later seven) *corps d'armée*. Their commanders included some of his most able and trusted subordinates. I Corps was led by the reliable **Marshal Claude Victor**. III Corps was commanded by **Marshal Bon-Adrien-Jeannot de Moncey**, who had been in Spain since the beginning of the year, but his fortunes had been mixed and he was subordinated to **Marshal Jean Lannes**, Napoleon's most trusted companion, who led Moncey's command to success at the Battle of Tudela in November and who took over the siege of Saragossa, Moncey being recalled in early January 1809. IV Corps was led by **Marshal François-Joseph Lefebvre**, who was removed in January 1809 after Napoleon commented, somewhat harshly, that 'he cannot read his instructions. It is impossible to entrust him with the command of a corps, which is a pity, as he shows great bravery on the field of battle'.[4] V Corps, led by **Marshal Edouard-Adolphe Mortier**, and VIII Corps, under **General Andoche Junot**, arrived in Spain only in December 1808, and Junot's Corps was broken up before the end of the year to reinforce other formations. VII Corps, led by **General Laurent Gouvion St. Cyr**, operated only in Catalonia. Also present in Spain was **Marshal Louis-Alexandre Berthier**, Napoleon's invaluable chief-of-staff.

9

The French commanders most involved in the Corunna campaign led the remaining two corps. VI Corps was led by **Marshal Michel Ney**, one of Napoleon's most stalwart and trusted lieutenants, though his corps was reduced in size when the campaign began. II Corps had been led by Napoleon's senior cavalry commander, **Marshal Jean-Baptiste Bessières.** He had won the Battle of Medina del Rio Seco (14 July 1808), although Napoleon considered his subsequent performance somewhat lethargic, and in early November 1808 Bessières was transferred to a position of rather less responsibility, command of the reserve cavalry. In his place Napoleon appointed **Marshal Jean-de-Dieu Soult**, who arrived in Spain from Berlin at a pace so furious that finally he even outdistanced his aides. Commissioned in 1792 and a general by 1794, Soult was one of Napoleon's most capable subordinates. He had led IV Corps of the *Grande Armée* at Austerlitz and Jena and in June 1808 had been ennobled as Duke of Dalmatia (from which title he was given his nickname 'Duke of Damnation' by the British). Napoleon described him as 'the ablest tactician in the empire', and he came to be admired even by his enemies – William Napier, for example, wrote that 'I take this opportunity to declare that respect which I believe every British officer who has had the honour to serve against him feels for his military talents'.[5] Wellington, however, identified a possible weakness, claiming that although Soult was most skilful in bringing his troops to the battlefield, once there he was never quite certain how to use them: 'a very able man – excellent as an *administrateur* but in the field he is apt to doubt and hesitate, and to lose the proper moment for acting'.

Emperor Napoleon I (1769–1821), wearing the uniform of the Chasseurs à Cheval of the Imperial Guard. (Print after Horace Vernet)

THE SPANISH

Administration in 'patriot' Spain was in the hands of a Supreme *Junta* to which the provincial *Juntas* or governments sent representatives. Its members included a considerable number of clerics and only five out of 35 had any military experience, and three of them only as militia officers. A Council of War convened at Madrid on 5 September, of the leading generals or their representatives, failed to appoint a commander-in-chief; and neither did the Supreme *Junta* when it elected its president and cabinet later in the month. Thus, while a common strategy was decided, the deficiency of a unified command was a serious flaw, and threw greater responsibility upon the various generals.

Towards the end of 1808 there were five principal armies opposing the French forces, with a 'front line' roughly along the Ebro river. At the eastern end of the line, in Catalonia, was the 'Army of the Right' under the aged **General Vives**, Captain-General in the Balearic Islands, and to his left the Reserve Army of **General José de Palafox y Melzi**, Captain-General of Aragon, who became greatly distinguished by his defence of Saragossa. Further west, holding the centre of the Spanish position, was the Army of the Centre under **General Francisco Xavier Castaños**, and to his left was the Army of Estremadura. Until 2 November this had been led by the Captain-General of that province, José Galuzzo, but he had been recalled by the Supreme *Junta* and command had devolved upon a young aristocrat of no military experience, the **Condé de Belvedere**. At the western end of the Spanish position was the Army of the Left, led by

Marshal Jean-Baptiste Bessières (1768–1813), original commander of Napoleon's II Corps, later commander of the Reserve Cavalry. (Engraving by Hopwood)

General Joaquin Blake, the Captain-General of Galicia, one of the better Spanish commanders, possessed of organisational ability and with a more realistic outlook than some, but limited as a field commander. The Spanish general most involved in the Corunna campaign, however, was **General Pedro Caro y Sureda, Marquis of La Romana**, who had commanded the Spanish expedition which had been sent to support Napoleon in the Baltic region, under the earlier alliance with Napoleon. They were in Denmark while the French were endeavouring to occupy Spain, but they remained loyal to the legitimate Spanish monarchy, revolted against the alliance with France and almost the whole force escaped upon a British fleet and was landed at Santander. Most joined Blake's army, and La Romana succeeded Blake in command in mid-November. La Romana was the Spanish general most esteemed by the British for his unswerving loyalty and his character; after his sudden death in 1811 Wellington described him as his country's 'most upright patriot … the most strenuous and zealous defender of the cause in which we are engaged'.[6] His military skill, however, received less praise; Wellington also remarked that 'I never in my whole life saw a man who had acted at all with troops understand so little about them'.

THE BRITISH

The central figure in the Corunna campaign was **Sir John Moore**. His appointment to lead expeditions to Sweden and to the Peninsula, despite his politics, was presumably because his talents were too great to ignore, and because of his support in the army. Although the government did support him and leave most matters in his hands, it was as uncomfortable with him as he was with the ministry. Indeed, although no criticism was made in public, such disquiet was felt in private that the Foreign Secretary, George Canning, suggested to the Prime Minister, Lord Portland, that Moore might be replaced in mid-campaign.

Moore's reputation as Britain's leading general was based upon his experiences in subordinate positions rather than success in independent commands in the field. The son of a Scottish doctor with high connections, he had been commissioned in 1776 and had seen much active service, and had served as a Member of Parliament in the interest of his friend the Duke of Hamilton. Despite being sent home from Corsica after a dispute with the viceroy, he retained the confidence of William Pitt and of the Duke of York, went to the West Indies as brigadier-general and gained distinction as a major-general in Ireland during the 1798 rebellion and when leading a brigade in Holland in 1799. He was his friend Abercrombie's most valuable subordinate in the Egyptian expedition, and in 1803 commanded at Shorncliffe, where he was instrumental in the development of light infantry tactics; although he was in no way exclusively responsible for this, it is as a trainer that he is perhaps best remembered. Lieutenant-general in 1805, he succeeded Henry Fox as commander in the Mediterranean, before the abortive expedition to Sweden.

If Moore were not popular with some members of the political and military establishment, he was a charismatic leader whose close subordinates regarded him with a devotion verging upon idolatry. George

**Sir John Hope, later 4th Earl of
Hopetoun (1765–1823), Moore's
reliable deputy who succeeded
to command of the army during
the Battle of Corunna.**

**William Beresford, later
1st Viscount Beresford
(1768–1854); one of Moore's
brigade commanders and
later Marshal of the Portuguese
Army. (Engraving after
Sir William Beechey)**

Napier was typical: 'In Sir John Moore's character we have a model for everything that marks the obedient soldier, the persevering, firm, and skilful general; the inflexible and real patriot who sacrificed all personal feeling to his country's weal; the truly virtuous and honourable man; the high-minded, finished, and accomplished gentleman'.[7] To John Colborne he was 'a most extraordinary man. The nearer you saw him, the more he was admired. He was superior by many degrees to everyone I have seen: he had a magnificent mind. A most perfect gentleman, a determined enemy to the corrupt … A man of this cast must create a host of enemies, and he certainly had his share of them'.[8] Moore also made an impression upon the ordinary soldiers; Charles Steevens, commanding the 20th Foot's light company, met him shortly before the Battle of Corunna and recalled that he 'made his enquiries and gave his orders to me in such a mild gentlemanly way; I was quite struck with his engaging manners, and so were my two subalterns; and I am sure the men of my company seemed, all of them, to be equally pleased with him'.[9]

The most senior of Moore's subordinates in the Corunna campaign was **Lieutenant-General Sir David Baird**, a tough Scot who had seen much active service in India and had survived three and a half years' dreadful imprisonment in Mysore. He gained his revenge by leading the storm of Seringapatam in 1799, commanded the Indian expedition to Egypt in 1801 and the expedition which captured the Cape, and led a division in the Danish expedition of 1807. However, he was probably not an easy subordinate, thinking himself ill-used and discriminated against, which led to his commander at Seringapatam, Lord Harris, to remark upon his 'total want of discretion and respect'.

Next senior was **Lieutenant-General Sir John Hope**, later 4th Earl of Hopetoun, another Scot of extensive experience, whose style of command was marked by taking risks with his personal safety. Wellington commented at a later date that 'I have long entertained the highest opinion of Sir John Hope, in common, I believe, with the whole world, but every day's experience convinces me of his worth. We shall lose him, however, if he continues to expose himself in fire … he places himself among the sharpshooters without, as they do, sheltering himself from the enemy's fire'.[10] Of Moore's other two divisional commanders the first, **Major-General Sir Edward Paget**, was a capable and resolute officer who was to be greatly distinguished by his command of the rearguard in the Corunna campaign, and though stern was popular and trusted by his men – as one remarked, he was 'an out and out good 'un' on the day of battle.[11] The second, **Lieutenant-General Alexander Mackenzie Fraser**, was another experienced commander, described as 'mild as a Lamb, and as a Lion strong'.[12]

The brigade commanders included a number of famous individuals, some of whom won greater fame under Wellington: Rowland Hill, later Wellington's most trusted subordinate; William Carr Beresford, later

RIGHT **Sir Thomas Graham, later 1st Baron Lynedoch (1748–1843),** a friend of Moore who accompanied him as an unofficial aide in the campaign. This later portrait shows him in the uniform of a lieutenant-general. (Print after Sir Thomas Lawrence)

FAR RIGHT **Rowland Hill, later 1st Viscount Hill (1772–1842);** a brigade commander in the Corunna campaign, he became Wellington's most trusted deputy in the later Peninsular war.

Henry William Paget, later 2nd Earl of Uxbridge and 1st Marquess of Anglesey (1768–1854); a skilled commander who led Moore's cavalry in the Corunna campaign.

commander of the Portuguese Army; James Leith, one of the soundest of Wellington's divisional commanders; the Hanoverian Charles Alten; and Robert Craufurd. Another was Coote Manningham, one of the founders of the British 95th Rifles, who died from the fatigues of the campaign in August 1809, aged only 44.

Moore's cavalry was commanded by Edward Paget's elder brother, **Lord Henry William Paget**, later Earl of Uxbridge and Marquess of Anglesey, who was to prove himself to be one of the best British cavalry leaders. His brigadiers were Charles William Stewart (later Marquess of Londonderry and Castlereagh's half-brother) and the ineffectual 'Jack' Slade. Moore's friend, the 60-year-old but enthusiastic Colonel Thomas Graham (later Lord Lynedoch), accompanied him as an aide in an unofficial capacity, and included in Moore's personal staff were two officers who subsequently rose to the rank of field marshal: his military secretary, John Colborne, who was to gain great distinction under Wellington, and Henry Hardinge, who became a distinguished Governor-General of India.

4 *Napoleon*. Vol.II p.11
5 W. Napier, Vol.I p.viii
(6 Wellington, Duke of, *Dispatches of Field-Marshal the Duke of Wellington*, ed. J. Gurwood, London 1834–8, Vol.VII p.190
7 G. Napier pp.77–78
8 Moore Smith, p.109
9 Steevens, p.76
10 Wellington, op. cit., Vol.XI pp.371–72
11 *Colburn's United Service Magazine* 1848, Vol.III p.29
12 *Gentleman's Magazine* October 1809, p.902

OPPOSING ARMIES

THE FRENCH

Although every French army of the period was a formidable force, especially with Napoleon himself at its head, that which he led in Spain was not quite the triumphant body which he had led in 1805–06. The troops already in Spain before Napoleon arrived had evidently suffered from their experience, as in August 1808 Joseph Bonaparte had reported to his brother that 'The soldiers are generally worn out, the officers are not strong, the men are young and raw … every officer going from Spain will tell the same story.'[13] Napoleon evidently believed that their morale must have been affected by the unimpressive performance of their commanders: 'Nothing has been done to give confidence to the French; there is not a soldier who does not see everything breathes timidity.'[14]

The enormous reinforcement which Napoleon led into Spain – about 130,000 strong – outnumbered the almost 100,000 already there, and included troops not only from the *Grande Armée* in Germany but from Italy and from the allied states of the Confederation of the Rhine. The entire Imperial Guard also went to Spain, the Fusiliers and cavalry already having been serving there, but a considerable proportion of the new troops were not the veterans which might have been expected from the **Grande Armée**. Napoleon had been compelled to conscript some 140,000 men, almost half below the usual age for service, and while most of these had been sent to Germany and Italy to replace the experienced men, a considerable proportion of Napoleon's army in Spain were new soldiers. Excluding units left behind in garrison, the field army in Spain in November 1808 included about 31 per cent of the infantry battalions, and 29 per cent of the cavalry regiments, which were either ad hoc 'provisional' regiments assembled from drafts, or foreigners. From July 1808 the provisional regiments were amalgamated and re-designated as line regiments, numbered from 114 onwards – thus in II Corps the 13th, 14th, 17th and 18th Provisional Regiments became the 119th and 120th Line, while the 122nd Line (which fought at Corunna) was formed from the 1st and 2nd Supplementary Regiments of the Legion of Reserve.

Napoleon's logistics problems were considerable. Although the administration was generally efficient, Napoleon was appalled by what he discovered in early November: 'You will see how shamefully I am treated; I have only 1400 coats, 7000 greatcoats instead of 50,000, 15,000 pairs of shoes instead of 129,000. I am in want of everything; nothing can be worse than the clothing. My army will begin the campaign naked; it has nothing. The conscripts are not clothed. Your reports are waste paper … My army is naked, just as it enters on a campaign. I have spent a great deal, which has been money thrown into the sea.'[15]

A fusilier of French line infantry, representative of the backbone of Napoleon's army in the Peninsula.

OPPOSITE **A *voltigeur* (left) and *carabinier* (right) of French light infantry, troops often in the van of the action during the Corunna campaign. (Engraving after Hippolyte Bellangé)**

Each of the **corps d'armée** was organised as a self-contained entity, with cavalry, artillery, and supporting services. The advantage of this was evident in Spain, where the considerable distances involved might otherwise have caused difficulties in support and reinforcement. The large area of campaign also exacerbated the difficulties of the gathering of intelligence and reconnaissance, a factor which bedevilled all the armies involved. As will be seen, for much of the time the commanding generals had to formulate their strategy without any real knowledge of the strength or location of their enemy.

FRENCH ARMY ORDER OF BATTLE

Napoleon's army in Spain, November 1808
I Corps (Victor): three divisions, 28,500 men
II Corps (Bessières): three divisions, 20,000 men
III Corps (Moncey): four divisions, 19,000 men
IV Corps (Lefebvre): three divisions, 20,000 men
V Corps (Mortier): two divisions, 22,500 men
VI Corps (Ney): two divisions, 20,000 men
VII Corps (St. Cyr): six divisions, 36,000 men
VIII Corps (Junot): three divisions, 20,000 men
Cavalry reserve: six divisions, 17,000 men
Imperial Guard: 12,000 men
Infantry reserve (including Joseph's Guard): 13,000 men
(These figures do not include detached units or the sick)

Orders of battle for the Corps most involved in the Corunna campaign
II Corps (Bessières; Soult from 9 November)
1st Division (Mouton; later Merle): 2me & 4me Léger, 15me & 36me Line (3 bns. each)
2nd Division (Merle; later Mermet): 31me Léger (3 btns.), 47me Line (2 bns.), 70me & 86me Line, 2me & 3me Swiss Regts. (1 bn. each), 122me Line (4 bns.)
3rd Division (Bonnet): 119me & 120me Line (4 bns. each) (detached from Corps in January 1809 as garrison of Santander)
Cavalry (Lasalle): 9me Dragoons, 10me & 22me Chasseurs à Cheval. Lasalle and all but the 22me were detached by mid–November and replaced by:
Franceschi's Division: 8me Dragoons, 1st Provisional & 22me Chasseurs à Cheval, Hanoverian Chevau-Légers. After the Sahagun losses the 1st Provisional Chasseurs was dissolved in January 1809 and replaced by the 1er Hussars.
After the disbanding of VIII Corps (December 1808) two new divisions were formed, incorporating some units from the existing divisions. For the new organisation, see the Corunna order of battle, plus:
4th Division (Heudelet): 15me Léger, 32me & 82me Line, Légion du Midi, Hanoverian Legion (1 bn. each); 26me & 66me Line (2 bns. each)

VI Corps (Ney)
1st Division (Marchand): 6me, 39me, 69me & 76me Line (3 bns. each)
2nd Division (Lagrange, later Maurice Mathieu): 25me Léger, 50me Line (4 bns. each), 27me & 59me Line (3 bns. each)
Cavalry (Colbert): 3me Hussars, 15me Chasseurs à Cheval

Napoleon's pursuing force
This included in addition to Ney's Corps the following:
Lapisse's Division (originally from I Corps): l6me Léger, 8me, 45me & 54me Line (3 bns. each)
Dessolle's Division: 12me Léger, 43me, 51me & 55me Line (3 bns. each)
Lahoussaye's & Lorges' cavalry divisions: (see Corunna order of battle)
Maupetit's cavalry division (from IV Corps): 5me Dragoons, 3rd Dutch Hussars, Westphalian Chevau-Légers
Imperial Guard: Grenadiers à Pied & Chasseurs à Pied (4 bns. each), Fusiliers (6 bns.), Chasseurs à Cheval, Grenadiers à Cheval, Dragoons, Gendarmerie d'Elite, Polish Chevau-Légers, Mamelukes

Soult's army at Corunna
1st Division (Merle) (brigades of Reynaud, Sarrut, Thomières): 2me Léger, 15me & 36me Line (3 bns. each), 4me Léger (4 bns.)
2nd Division (Mermet) (brigades of Gaulois, Jardon, Lefebvre): 31me Léger, 47me & 122me Line (4 bns. each). Evidently the 2nd & 3rd Swiss Regts. (total 3 bns.) had been detached

RIGHT **French troops on the march in the Peninsula; during the pursuit of Moore the weather was generally very much worse than that shown here. (Print after Maurice Orange)**

3rd Division (Delaborde) (brigades of Foy and Arnaud): 17me Léger, 86me Line (3 bns. each), 70me Line (4 bns.). The 4th Swiss Regt. (1 bn.) had been detached

Lahoussaye's Dragoon Division (brigades of Marisy & Caulaincourt): 17me, 18me, 19me & 27me Dragoons

Lorges' Dragoon Division (brigades of Vialannes & Fournier): 13me, 15me, 22me & 25me Dragoons

Franceschi's Division: ler Hussars, 8me Dragoons, 22me Chasseurs à Cheval, Hanoverian Chevau-Légers (detached from the army).

THE SPANISH

Representatives of the Spanish Army: light infantry (left) and artillery (right). (Engraving by Clark after Rev. William Bradford, a military chaplain who served in the Corunna campaign)

Napoleon's opinion that the Spanish armies were the worst in Europe was echoed by many of the British who encountered them in the Corunna campaign. William Surtees, for example, thought them 'nothing better than mere rabble – no organization, no subordination, but every one evidently pursued that plan which seemed right in his own eyes … they, in their best days, are more like an armed mob than regularly organised soldiers'.[16] Such statements, however, were a reflection upon administration and leadership rather than upon the character of the soldiers. Spanish armies were often hastily raised, ill-trained and badly equipped, with ineffective leadership. Surtees remarked that 'Nothing could exceed the hardy and robust appearance of the men in general; and had they been clothed, appointed, and disciplined like either their enemies or their allies, there could not have been a finer soldiery.'[17] Robert Blakeney was another who encountered them in the Corunna campaign: 'Courage was never wanting to the Spanish soldiers; but confidence in their chiefs was rare … [many] were

left barefoot, ragged and half-starved. In this deplorable state they were brought into the field under leaders many of whom were scarcely competent to command a sergeant's outlying piquet ... injustice and neglect powerfully tend to damp and dispirit the ardour even of the most zealous and devoted.'[18]

Although many of the Spanish armies in the field performed unimpressively in 1808, the civilian population was capable of great feats of endurance and courage, as shown by the siege of Saragossa. Yet innumerable British participants in the Corunna campaign commented upon the lack of co-operation they received. They had understood that the whole country was prepared to take up arms, or at least to assist those who were actively opposing the French, but they were disappointed. In his letter of 13 January 1809 to Castlereagh, Moore commented that the 'apathy and indifference of the Spaniards would never have been believed', and that 'it was necessary to risk this army to convince the people of England, as well as the rest of Europe, that the Spaniards had neither the power nor the inclination to make any effort for themselves'. Sir John Tylden of the 43rd was another who articulated the general perception: 'Some few have behaved with civility, but the greater number treat us as intruders, not as people coming to defend them ... I begin most heartily to hate the whole of them; they are not worth the trouble of fighting for, and I wish I was now in England'. He was even among those who excused British plundering by stating that 'the inhabitants, by their refusal of the necessaries of life, even for money, and by their brutal behaviour have brought it greatly on themselves'.[19] No matter how misguided and unjust were such opinions of the Spanish in general, some unfortunate experiences during the campaign led to them being held by many of the British, which unavoidably coloured their perception of events.

French Chasseurs à Cheval crossing a ford, led by their regimental *élite* company, recognisable by their distinctive fur caps. Such troops generally formed the vanguard of advancing forces. (Print after H. Chartier)

THE BRITISH

Moore's army was not just the largest that Britain had in the field, it was virtually the only army available. William Napier commented that Moore was conscious that 'not an English army, but the very heart, the pith of the military power of his country was in his keeping [and] was entrusted to his prudence',[20] and it is against this huge responsibility that all Moore's actions should be gauged.

Unlike the French forces, which had a large proportion of experienced campaigners, comparatively few of the British units had any recent experience of campaigning. Of the 35 infantry battalions, only 15 had served with Wellesley at Vimeiro (when it was remarked that some suffered considerably from lack of experience), and in the final organisation four of the eleven brigades contained not a single battalion of even this experience. For example, of the eight battalions in the 1st Division, only one (50th) had fought at Vimeiro, one had last seen active service in Egypt in 1801 (42nd), two had been raised within the previous five years and had seen no active service (1st, 81st) and the remainder only had experience of somewhat unchallenging duties in Hanover, Sicily and Copenhagen. Of the cavalry regiments, three had

A British 15th Hussar loading his carbine. (Engraving by I.C. Stadler after Charles Hamilton Smith)

last seen active service in Holland in 1799, one had been raised in 1806 and had served at Copenhagen, and one had last seen active service in the Seven Years War. The fact that much of the army was unused to the brutal realities of very hard campaigning must have contributed considerably to the breakdown in discipline and cohesion during the retreat to Corunna.

Somewhat unusually, Moore radically altered the organisation of his army in mid-campaign, in which only five of the original brigades remained unchanged. At various stages during the campaign these forces were not totally in a complete body, with some units joining the army relatively late in the operations and others failing to join at all. An extreme case is provided by the 1/3rd Buffs, which was intended to form a brigade with the 1/50th under Moore Disney, but which was instead broken up into detachments to escort convoys en route to the army. In the event, only one company actually joined Moore, on about 24 December, the remainder (escorting a large sum of money intended for Moore's use) eventually retiring to Oporto when it became obvious that they could not catch him up. This caused great anxiety on the part of the staff in Portugal who for some weeks had no idea where they were!

BRITISH ARMY ORDER OF BATTLE
Original organisation:
(Note: 1/9th designates 1st Btn. 9th Regt., etc.)

Moore's contingent
Beresford's Bde.: 1/9th (East Norfolk), 2/43rd (Monmouthshire Light Infantry),
    2/52nd (Oxfordshire Light Infantry)
Fane's Bde.: 1/38th (1st Staffordshire), 1/79th (Cameron Highlanders), 4 coys. 2/95th Rifles
Bentinck's Bde.: 1/4th (King's Own), 1/28th (North Gloucestershire), 1/42nd (Royal Highland), 4 coys.
    5/60th (Royal American)
Hill's Bde.: 1/5th (Northumberland), 1/32nd (Cornwall), 1/91st (Argyllshire Highlanders)
Anstruther's Bde.: 20th (East Devonshire), 1/52nd (Oxfordshire Light Infantry), 5 coys. 1/95th Rifles
Alten's Bde.: 1st & 2nd Light Bns., King's German Legion
Artillery: Wilmot's company

Hope's contingent
18th (King's) Hussars, 3rd King's German Legion Hussars, 2nd (Queen's Royal), 1/36th (Herefordshire),
    1/71st (Glasgow Highland), 1/92nd (Gordon Highlanders), 5 coys. 5/60th (Royal American)
Artillery: Carthew's, Crawford's, Drummond's & Raynsford's companies, plus Skyring's &
    Thornhill's companies as depot and park, without guns

Baird's contingent
Cavalry (Lord Paget): 7th (Queen's Own), 10th (Prince of Wales's Own) & 15th (King's) Hussars
1st (Warde's) Bde.: 1/1st & 3/1st Foot Guards
2nd (Manningham's) Bde.: 3/1st (Royals), 1/26th (Cameronians), 2/81st
3rd (Leith's) Bde.: 51st (2nd Yorkshire West Riding), 2/59th (2nd Nottinghamshire), 76th (Hindoostan)
Light (Craufurd's) Bde.: 1/43rd (Monmouthshire Light Infantry), 5 coys. 1/95th Rifles, 4 coys. 2/95th Rifles.
    Latterly the 2/14th (Bedfordshire) and 2/23rd (Royal Welch Fuzileers) were also under Craufurd 's
    command
Artillery: Downman's & Evelagh's horse artillery troops; Bean's, Truscott's, Wall's & Holcombe's
    companies, of which the latter was evidently left at Corunna
(Of the artillery employed in the campaign, Raynsford's company was equipped with 9-pdrs, the rest with
    light 6-pdrs)
Other units joined the army. The 3/27th (Inniskilling) and 2/31st (Huntingdonshire) were sent to Lisbon,
    releasing the 1/3rd (Buffs) and 1/50th (West Kent) for service with Moore. The latter joined Moore, but
    the Buffs were used as convoy escorts and ultimately retired to Portugal, though the grenadier
    company, the quartermaster and one additional ensign did join the field army and were attached to the
    20th from 2 January. The 5/60th contained so many French ex-prisoners of war that the battalion was
    regarded as untrustworthy, so Hope sent his companies back to Lisbon, and Moore sent his to
    Almeida, where they relieved the 1/6th (1st Warwickshire) which joined the army. The 1/82nd (Prince of
    Wales's Volunteers) was the last battalion to leave Lisbon and eventually caught up with the army, but
    the remainder of its brigade, the 1/45th (Nottinghamshire) and 97th (Queen's Own Germans), never
    joined the main force

Riflemen of the British 95th, in their distinctive dark green uniforms. (Print after J.A. Atkinson)

ARMEE.

A British baggage wagon loaded with a regiment's equipment, soldiers' wives and children. Most of Moore's transport was hired in the Peninsula but this gives some indication of the difficulty of transportation over poor roads. (Engraving after W.H. Pyne)

The force left behind in Portugal, to garrison Lisbon, Almeida and Elvas, ultimately commanded by Sir John Cradock, included in addition to those units mentioned above the 20th Light Dragoons; 2/9th (East Norfolk); 29th (Worcestershire); 1/40th (2nd Somersetshire), the 1st, 2nd, 5th & 7th Line Bns., King's German Legion; Bredin's and Lawson's artillery companies and Nos. 1, 2 and 4 Coys., King's German Legion Artillery, with three batteries of light 6-pdrs, one of 12-pdrs and one of 3-pdrs The 2/60th landed at Corunna in November 1808 and remained there in garrison

Moore's army as reorganised at Mayorqa
Cavalry (Lord Paget): Slade's Bde.: 10th & 15th Hussars
   Stewart's Bde.: 7th, 18th & 3rd KGL Hussars
   Artillery: Downman's & Evelagh's troops
1st Division (Baird): Warde's Bde.: 1/1st & 3/1st Foot Guards
   Bentinck's Bde.: 1/4th, 1/42nd, 1/50th
   Manningham's Bde.: 3/1st, 1/26th, 2/81st
   Artillery: Bean's company
2nd Division (Hope): Leith's Bde.: 51st, 2/59th, 76th
   Hill's Bde.: 2nd, 1/5th, 2/14th, 1/32nd
   Catlin Craufurd's Bde.: 1/36th, 1/71st, 1/92nd
   Artillery: Drummond's company
3rd Division (Fraser): Beresford's Bde.: 1/6th, 1/9th, 2/23rd, 2/43rd
   Fane's Bde.: 1/38th, 1/79th, 1/82nd
   Artillery: Wilmot's company
Reserve Division (Edward Paget): Anstruther's Bde.: 20th, 1/52nd, 1/95th
   Disney's Bde.: 1/28th, 1/91st
   Artillery: Carthew's company
1st Flank Bde. (Robert Craufurd): 1/43rd, 2/52nd, 2/95th
2nd Flank Bde. (Alten): 1st & 2nd KGL Light Bns.
Artillery reserve (LtCol John Harding): the remaining five companies.

13 Napoleon, Vol.I p.342
14 ibid., Vol.I p.363
15 ibid., Vol.I pp.370–71
16 Surtees, pp.77, 92
17 ibid., p.108
18 Blakeney, pp.311, 313
19 Tylden, pp.131–32, 142
20 W. Napier, Vol.I p.427

THE CAMPAIGN

MOORE'S ADVANCE

Although the purpose of the intended British operation was clear – to support the Spanish armies – the exact manner in which it might be achieved was a matter of debate. Various plans were considered by the ministry, including a highly impractical scheme for the British army to be landed in northern Spain to operate against the French flank and rear. When Moore was given his command in Portugal, it was evidently intended that he would transfer his army from Lisbon to Corunna by sea, with Galicia providing a secure base from which to advance into Spain. At Corunna, Moore would be reinforced, and then advance into Old Castile, to the region around Burgos, to support the Spanish Armies of the Left and Centre.

In the event, Moore decided not to follow the ministry's intended plan of campaign, but to advance overland from Portugal instead. This manoeuvre certainly placed his army in danger, but certain factors made the alternative plan equally difficult. The army's commissariat organisation was so imperfect and inexperienced that great reliance would have to be placed upon the resources of the country, both for supplies and the means of transporting them, but Galicia was an impoverished province which might not be able to support an army. Its administration, also, was not inclined to be especially co-operative, as Baird discovered when he landed at Corunna (although this fact would not have been known to Moore when he was formulating his plan of campaign). The transportation of troops from Lisbon to Corunna by sea could have been disrupted by bad weather, for which that part of the coast was renowned in that late season of the year, and the alternative of a coastal march to Corunna would have been hazardous, as the roads northwards were unknown to Moore. He also remarked that the disruption caused by embarkation and disembarkation would greatly delay the campaign, a delay which might prove fatal. Finally, plans had already been laid for a more direct march into Spain, and some units were already actually in motion.

Although Moore's preferred option promised to render more rapid assistance to the Spanish armies, it would mean that his own army, marching from Lisbon, and the reinforcement under Sir David Baird which was being sent to Corunna, would remain separate for some time, although the two would have to unite before any major battle was contemplated. A more serious concern was the fact that, despite their long presence in Portugal, Moore's predecessors had made little attempt to survey the roads which would be used for such an advance, so that Moore was unsure which roads were suitable for the passage of artillery. Even the road to Almeida was unreported, despite the fact that British

Sir John Cradock, later 1st Baron Howden (1762–1839), who took command in Portugal after Moore advanced into Spain. (Print after Sir Thomas Lawrence)

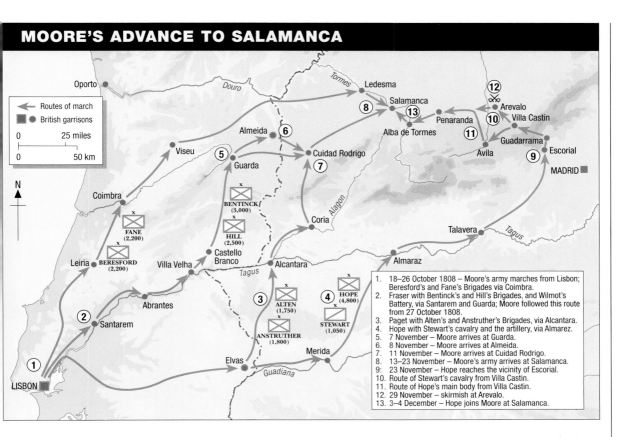

Oporto

Routes of march
British garrisons

0 25 miles
0 50 km

N

Douro
Tormes
Ledesma
Salamanca ⑧ ⑬
Penaranda ⑪
Alba de Tormes
⑫
Arevalo
Villa Castin ⑩
Avila ⑨ Escorial
Guadarrama
MADRID

Viseu
Almeida ⑥
Cuidad Rodrigo
⑤ Guarda ⑦

Coimbra

BENTINCK (3,000)

FANE (2,200)

HILL (2,500)

Coria

Alagon

Talavera

BERESFORD (2,200)
Leiria
Castello Branco
Villa Velha
Alcantara
Almaraz

Tagus
Tagus

Abrantes

② Santarem

③ ALTEN (1,750)
ANSTRUTHER (1,800)

④ HOPE (4,800)
STEWART (1,050)

Merida

Elvas
Guadiana

① LISBON

1. 18–26 October 1808 – Moore's army marches from Lisbon; Beresford's and Fane's Brigades via Coimbra.
2. Fraser with Bentinck's and Hill's Brigades, and Wilmot's Battery, via Santarem and Guarda; Moore followed this route from 27 October 1808.
3. Paget with Alten's and Anstruther's Brigades, via Alcantara.
4. Hope with Stewart's cavalry and the artillery, via Almarez.
5. 7 November – Moore arrives at Guarda.
6. 8 November – Moore arrives at Almeida.
7. 11 November – Moore arrives at Cuidad Rodrigo.
8. 13–23 November – Moore's army arrives at Salamanca.
9. 23 November – Hope reaches the vicinity of Escorial.
10. Route of Stewart's cavalry from Villa Castin.
11. Route of Hope's main body from Villa Castin.
12. 29 November – skirmish at Arevalo.
13. 3–4 December – Hope joins Moore at Salamanca.

Charles William Stewart, later 3rd Marquess of Londonderry (1778–1854), who led the cavalry of Hope's contingent in its advance. (Engraving by W.L. Colls after Sir Thomas Lawrence)

troops had marched along it to reach that fortress. Furthermore, the need to draw some of the army's provisions from the country meant that the army would have to advance by more than one route. Moore's predecessor, Dalrymple, had sent the capable Lord William Bentinck to liaise with the Spanish authorities in Madrid, but little intelligence of use had been obtained. Not only was no advice forthcoming about the routes of advance, but no coherent idea could be gleaned of the Spanish strategy. With no overall military commander with whom to confer, the *Junta* directed Bentinck to liaise with Castaños, but he could only speak for his own army. The apparent lack of central direction of the Spanish war effort, which must have been reported to the British government by its various military missions, may have been one reason why their preferred option was a concentration in Galicia, a rather more cautious plan than that adopted by Moore. Although it might be argued that Moore was given a near-impossible task, it is not unreasonable to add that the precise nature of the difficulties he faced were not of the ministry's making, but resulted from his own decision not to follow the suggested strategy but to follow his own plan, with which the ministry certainly acquiesced.

It was intended that the British Army should move into the line beside Blake and Castaños, along the line of the river Ebro, and Burgos was thus named as the approximate objective of the British advance. It was very near the front line, but at the time the plans were formulated, it was not envisaged that Napoleon would come to Spain with massive reinforcements and initiate an immediate offensive. Accordingly, Moore got his forces in motion with scarcely any delay, despite the huge **23**

difficulties presented by the lack of an efficient system of commissariat and transport. Even with these difficulties, however, they might have concentrated at Salamanca earlier than they did, in which case they could have supported the Spanish in their attempts to resist Napoleon's offensive; but in that case they would probably have been destroyed with no other achievement than causing Napoleon a temporary delay. As William Napier commented, Moore was 'too late in the field. The campaign was decided against the Spaniards before the British had, strictly speaking, entered Spain as an army'[21] and that the consequence of an earlier arrival would have been grave. However providential the delay proved for the British, it had unfortunate political consequences, allowing some Spaniards to raise doubts about the commitment of their ally.

The reason for the delay lay in the routes chosen for the advance into Spain. Moore intended to march on Almeida by three routes: the most northerly by Coimbra and Celorico, the middle route by Abrantes, Castello Branco and Guarda, and the most southerly by Elvas, Alcantara and Coria. The latter, neither the most direct nor easiest road, had to be used because two brigades were already at Elvas, and because Alcantara provided a bridge over the Tagus. Moore reduced his baggage to a minimum (though unfortunately permitted soldiers' wives and children to accompany the army, the cause of much misery later in the campaign), but roads were needed that were practicable for some heavy baggage and the artillery. In the event, the course of the campaign was determined by doubts over the actual state of the roads into Spain. Moore consulted the Portuguese Army, and those of Dalrymple's officers who supposedly knew the area, and was assured that neither the Coimbra nor Guarda roads were fit for artillery, despite the fact that a practicable road must have been necessary for the transportation of supplies to the major fortress of Almeida.

Faced with this intelligence, Moore had little choice but to send his artillery (but for one battery), with a strong escort and all his cavalry, under Hope, by a long and circuitous route which involved marching

Strategy was dictated by such river crossings as the bridge over the Tagus at Alcantara (in Arabic, 'the bridge', named from the famous Roman bridge built c. AD 105 in honour of Trajan). It was partially destroyed by the British in 1809. (Print after Robert Ker Porter)

British artillery being hauled inland just after disembarkation, with the assistance of naval personnel; Baird's landing at Corunna involved many difficulties, notably the local bureaucracy rather than the terrain. (Print after Thomas Rowlandson)

east from Elvas, crossing the Tagus at Almaraz, and continuing east until almost within the environs of Madrid, before turning north and west to approach Salamanca from the opposite direction to that taken by the rest of the army. The use of this main Elvas–Madrid road, although obviously suitable for the heavy load of the artillery, extended the march by more than one-third (Lisbon–Salamanca via Coimbra was 250 miles; Hope had to traverse 380). The resulting delay in the concentration of the army was between two and three weeks, and as all the cavalry and almost all the artillery was with Hope, it was impossible for Moore to consider an offensive movement before the two bodies united. It was especially unfortunate because the Coimbra road proved suitable for artillery, and Moore himself, who took the Castello Branco–Guarda route into Spain, found that his single battery of 6-pdrs travelled without difficulty; only when the weather worsened and turned the roads into mud did he report that wheeled transport was in difficulty.

Moore sent off his leading units as early as 11 October, had most of the army in motion by the 18th, and left Lisbon himself on the 26th. The brigades of Beresford and Henry Fane marched by the Coimbra route; Fraser led the brigades of Bentinck and Hill (and Wilmot's battery of light 6-pdrs) by Abrantes and Guarda (they were followed, rather later, by the 1/50th); while Edward Paget led the brigades of Alten and Robert Anstruther via Elvas and Alcantara. The march was unpleasant, through bad weather and with some shortage of supplies (a Portuguese contractor went bankrupt and reneged on his undertaking to supply them!), and some men died of dysentery on the march; but the first troops arrived at the principal destination, Salamanca, on 13 November, and most of Moore's own contingent was assembled there by the 23rd.

Baird's Advance

Hope's long march was not the only reason for Moore's delay. The reinforcement under Sir David Baird sailed into Corunna on 13 October, but found it impossible to land. Perhaps to avoid having to provide supplies, the local Galician *Junta* claimed that it had no authority to permit Baird to land, and suggested that he go instead to Santander. Baird declined this impractical suggestion and insisted that permission to land be sought from the Supreme *Junta*; this process took so long that not until 26 October did disembarkation begin, and the infantry was not all ashore until 4 November. Even then, the *Junta* would only permit the army to land in small detachments, and then to advance progressively into Castile, rather than allowing the whole force to concentrate and advance en masse, as Baird had intended; ostensibly this was to facilitate the provision of supplies in a region already denuded of resources by the Spanish armies.

The problem of supplies was critical, for Baird had little cash with which to purchase any, and little money could be raised by British government promissory notes. Generously, the Galician *Junta* loaned him 92,000 dollars – about £25,000 – and a further £40,000 was given him by the new British minister to Spain, John Hookham Frere, who arrived at Corunna with a large sum intended to help Spain finance the war. Even so, it was only with difficulty that Baird was able to procure supplies and transport for his advance towards a junction with Moore. There was yet another reason for delay; Baird's cavalry, the resource most required by Moore, had been late in leaving Britain, and not until 13 November was the whole of the cavalry, and their two troops of horse artillery, landed at Corunna. By 22 November, still without his cavalry, Baird had advanced to Astorga when he received dire news of Spanish defeats, and realised that there was no longer a Spanish army between himself and the French, who might therefore fall upon him as he marched towards Moore at Salamanca. Halting at Astorga, he sent the news to Moore and prepared to fall back upon Corunna.

NAPOLEON'S OFFENSIVE

The news which so shocked Baird was the result of Napoleon's determination to force the Spanish line along the river Ebro. With Lefebvre's IV Corps holding Blake on the Spanish left, and Moncey's III Corps containing Castaños and Palafox on the right, he intended to drive into the Spanish centre, upon Burgos and then south to Madrid, with his main body (Bessières' II Corps, Ney's VI Corps, the Imperial Guard, Joseph's reserve and the cavalry). Victor's newly arrived I Corps was to attempt to outflank Blake. Once the Spanish centre had been forced, Ney was to turn east and assist Moncey in driving Castaños and Palafox north and east, while Bessières was to turn west and assist in the defeat and pursuit of Blake. Napoleon's own force, reinforced by Mortier's V Corps which was still to arrive, would go on to Madrid. Even though Napoleon was not certain of exactly which Spanish force lay in his path, and had no knowledge whatever of the presence of British troops in Spain, it was a formidable plan, to be executed by overwhelming force against an unco-ordinated opponent.

ABOVE **The bridge over the river Agueda at Barba del Puerco. The scene of a famous skirmish in 1810, it exemplifies some of the difficulties encountered due to the nature of the roads taken by Moore on his advance into Spain. (Ian Fletcher Battlefield Tours)**

RIGHT **The river Agueda from the bridge at Barba del Puerco, showing the formidable nature of the terrain. (Ian Fletcher Battlefield Tours)**

Although Lefebvre began his attack before the other French forces were ready (31 October), the first decisive action occurred at Espinosa (10–11 November), where Blake's army, after a creditable defence, was routed by Victor. Napoleon's own offensive began when he arrived at Vittoria on 6 November. He ordered Bessières' II Corps to lead the advance upon Burgos, as the vanguard of a striking-force of almost 70,000 men, but his advance was tentative and on 9 November he was replaced by Soult, just arrived from Germany, with Bessières being transferred to command the reserve cavalry. It was thus Soult who led the attack against the Condé de Belvedere's small army, basically only two divisions of the Army of Estremadura, comparatively few of them regulars, and less than 11,000 in number. On 10 November the inexperienced young Spanish general was routed at Gamonal.

Burgos was taken, and Napoleon launched his flanking movements, Soult turning north-west to join the pursuit of Blake, Ney east against Castaños. By forced marches and in appalling conditions, Blake retired westwards and outdistanced his pursuers, but his army was temporarily wrecked and he was replaced in command by La Romana. As Soult followed, Victor and Lefebvre were instructed to join the southward march against Madrid. On the other flank of Napoleon's thrust, the corps of Moncey and Ney, commanded overall by Lannes, routed the army of Castaños at the Tudela (23 November) and that general was subsequently removed from his command.

With the enemy forces on either side in retreat – Palafox fell back on Saragossa, Castaños' army made a futile attempt to cover Madrid – Napoleon's flanks were secure for his advance on the capital, which he commenced in earnest on 28 November, on receiving news of Lannes' victory at the Tudela. The *Junta* did not attempt to do very much to concentrate resources for the defence of Madrid: Moore was only 150 miles away, Hope even nearer on his circuitous march, but the *Junta* still preferred to advise Moore to unite with what remained of Blake's army, further north. Thus, only some 12,000 Spanish troops, under General Benito San Juan, blocked the Somosierra pass through the mountains which shielded Madrid to the north. On 30 November Napoleon forced the position, and the road to Madrid lay open.

Moore's dilemma

By 23 November Moore was at Salamanca with some 15,000 infantry and one battery; Hope was near Madrid, at El Escorial, and about to march westwards again to effect his junction with Moore. Baird was at Astorga with part of his contingent, with the rest, including the cavalry, still on the march from Corunna. With the British forces so separated, there was no possibility of immediate action, yet morale was high, as Capt James Seaton of the 92nd remarked: 'There is no doubt but Bonaparte is in Spain. *So much the better*, we all say. We expect a general engagement … we are all anxious for it and in the highest possible spirits.'[22] Like Baird, Moore had learned of the Spanish defeats, knew that nothing shielded him from the French, and realised that if Napoleon marched westwards he would have to order his three columns to retire as best they could, before they could unite. By this time he probably realised that not much help could be rendered by the Spanish, with their failings in central direction and military leadership, and similar opinions were expressed in

Napoleon on campaign, in the snow, protected by members of the Grenadiers à Pied of the Imperial Guard. (Engraving by L. Roer after Jean-Louis Meisonnier)

correspondence from Bentinck and from Charles Stuart, temporary British minister with the *Junta*. Robert Ker Porter, who was with Moore's army, probably expressed a common perception when he remarked that the 'Spanish patriots' seemed to be 'sleeping on their arms'.[23] Despite the heavy responsibility of having to conserve Britain's only field army, Moore still hoped to assist the Spanish, as he had been instructed, until he received a crucial piece of information. Had he relied upon Spanish sources, it might have been many days before he received news of the Spanish defeat on the Tudela; but Stuart's secretary, Charles Vaughan, rode some 476 miles in six days, from the Tudela to Madrid and thence to Moore at Salamanca, carrying the news.

When Moore received it, on the night on 28 November, he issued orders for the retreat of his entire force immediately. Baird he ordered to return to Corunna, and then to go by sea to Lisbon; the indefatigable Vaughan carried the order to Baird at Astorga, where he arrived on 30 November, whereupon the general fell back upon Villafranca, leaving his light brigade and cavalry as a rearguard. Moore ordered Hope to march west towards Ciudad Rodrigo and Almeida, adding by way of explanation that he had been prepared to run great risks to aid the Spanish cause, 'but they have shown themselves equal to do so little for themselves, that it would only be sacrificing the army, without doing any good to Spain, to oppose such numbers as must now be brought against us'.[24] Moore, however, delayed his own retreat until Hope should be out of danger. In fact, although they had approached within 18 miles of

General Jean-Andoche Junot, Duc d'Abrantès (1771–1813), whose VIII Corps was hurried forward to support Soult, before being dispersed, with some troops being added to Soult's command. (Engraving by T. Read)

Hope's outposts, the French can have had no knowledge of the presence of so large a British force so near, and Hope's convoy was able to march westwards to safety. At Alba de Tormes, some 15 miles from Salamanca, Moore ordered him north instead of continuing west towards Ciudad Rodrigo, and so on 3 December Moore was united with his artillery at Salamanca, raising his force to about 20,000 men.

Moore's decision to retreat had been announced to his generals on 29 November, evidently to universal dismay. Charles Stewart, who had commanded Hope's cavalry, recalled how Moore had told him that the meeting with his generals was 'for the purpose of acquainting them with his decision … but he had neither requested their opinions, nor demanded their judgment', and that 'a choice of evils alone remained for him. The determination to which he had at last come, was not formed without extreme pain to himself; but the duty of preserving his army, situated as it now was, presented to his mind a consideration paramount to every other; he was, therefore, resolved to retreat.' Stewart expressed his misgivings, as did the other officers: 'Seldom did men, situated as we were, venture to speak out so boldly against the measures of their chief. But murmurings and remonstrances were useless; the die was cast and it could not be recalled.'[25]

In the event, the die was recalled. While he waited for Hope, various messages urged Moore to take action. On 30 November La Romana, that most stalwart and determined of Spanish commanders, wrote to report that he was at Leon, in command of what remained of Blake's army, and that although his men were ill-equipped and starving, their morale was buoyant. Envoys from the *Junta* arrived to beg Moore to march in defence of Madrid, but their case was undermined by the fact that they grossly under-estimated the strength of Napoleon's army, and were unaware of Napoleon's victory at Somosierra. (Moore had received this news from his friend Thomas Graham, who had left San Juan shortly after his defeat and just before he was murdered by his own troops!) If their entreaties did little to alter Moore's opinion, other matters did.

More decisive were despatches from Madrid, from the '*Junta* of Defence', sent on 2 December. They wrote of the threat to the capital from Napoleon's advance, and stated that its citizens were determined to defend it; and implied that Moore could assist that defence by threatening Napoleon's flank and rear. Hope's intelligence, which suggested that no French forces were pushing westwards but were all evidently heading for Madrid, must also have suggested to Moore the possibility of attacking their communications. Probably more telling was an appeal from the British minister Frere, whose concern was the political damage which would be done if Moore retired and was thought to have abandoned the Spaniards. In this, Frere was probably correct, especially if the British had retreated at a time when the citizens of Madrid were mobilising to resist Napoleon; but he proved himself probably unfit for the post he held by writing a second document on the subject, which apparently was a deliberate attempt to undermine Moore's authority. Even Frere's choice of envoy was contentious, as his despatches to Moore were carried by one Col Venault de Charmilly, an untrustworthy *émigré* of bad reputation. The second document – described by William Napier as 'a foolish, wanton insult'[26] – was to request that Charmilly be allowed to put Frere's argument to a Council

of War, in effect appealing to Moore's subordinates to overrule their general. Given the discontent in the army, it could have provoked much argument, and was disloyal to the military commander who should have been able to rely on Frere's support. It led to Moore having Charmilly thrown out of his camp when the second document was delivered.

Ironically, it need never have been delivered, for the first, with the other intelligence which suggested that Madrid was preparing to fight, had changed Moore's mind. The prospect of leaving Madrid to its fate, and abandoning the cause for which his army had been despatched, was too much, and consequently Moore wrote to Baird, late on 5 December, ordering him to cancel his retreat on Corunna and instead advance into Leon. Moore was under no illusions about the dangers involved; on the following day he wrote to Baird that the fate of Madrid might be decisive, and that they had to make an effort, while recognising that 'I mean to proceed bridle in hand, for, if the bubble bursts, we shall have a run for it'.[27] Although it would result in the uniting of Moore's army with his own, Baird perhaps had no great confidence in it: an officer who had been away scouting recorded that on his return Baird remarked, 'I'm glad the responsibility is off my shoulders. In fact, Sir J. Moore seems to have been driven to this unhappy movement by the importunities of Mr. Frere.'[28]

After the various delays, it was somewhat ironic that even before Moore had decided to act, the object of his advance was lost. On 3 December Napoleon captured the Retiro heights overlooking Madrid, and on the following day, faced with the prospect of a bloody assault, the Spanish opened the gates of their city, and Napoleon took it unopposed.

THE ADVANCE TO SAHAGUN

Moore's intention was to strike at French communications by advancing upon Valladolid or Burgos, forcing Napoleon to turn against him and thus relieve pressure upon Madrid. He reckoned that the French were not sufficiently strong to overwhelm the 29,000 men he would have when united with Baird, believing that Napoleon had about 80,000 men in Spain (excluding those in Catalonia), whereas Napoleon had more

The battlefield of Sahagun. At the time of the action its appearance was very different, covered with snow and in the half-light of dawn. (Ian Fletcher Battlefield Tours)

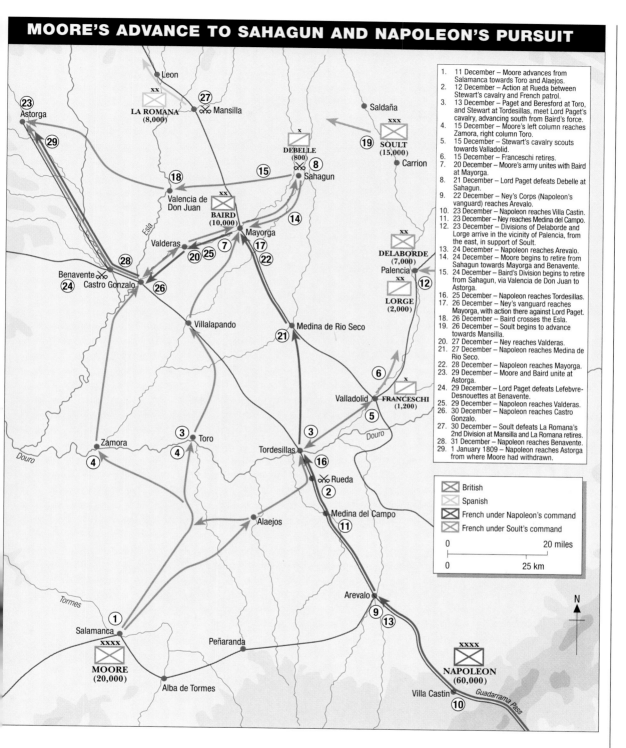

1. 11 December – Moore advances from Salamanca towards Toro and Alaejos.
2. 12 December – Action at Rueda between Stewart's cavalry and French patrol.
3. 13 December – Paget and Beresford at Toro, and Stewart at Tordesillas, meet Lord Paget's cavalry, advancing south from Baird's force.
4. 15 December – Moore's left column reaches Zamora, right column Toro.
5. 15 December – Stewart's cavalry scouts towards Valladolid.
6. 15 December – Franceschi retires.
7. 20 December – Moore's army unites with Baird at Mayorga.
8. 21 December – Lord Paget defeats Debelle at Sahagun.
9. 22 December – Ney's Corps (Napoleon's vanguard) reaches Arevalo.
10. 23 December – Napoleon reaches Villa Castin.
11. 23 December – Ney reaches Medina del Campo.
12. 23 December – Divisions of Delaborde and Lorge arrive in the vicinity of Palencia, from the east, in support of Soult.
13. 24 December – Napoleon reaches Arevalo.
14. 24 December – Moore begins to retire from Sahagun towards Mayorga and Benavente.
15. 24 December – Baird's Division begins to retire from Sahagun, via Valencia de Don Juan to Astorga.
16. 25 December – Napoleon reaches Tordesillas.
17. 26 December – Ney's vanguard reaches Mayorga, with action there against Lord Paget.
18. 26 December – Baird crosses the Esla.
19. 26 December – Soult begins to advance towards Mansilla.
20. 27 December – Ney reaches Valderas.
21. 27 December – Napoleon reaches Medina de Rio Seco.
22. 28 December – Napoleon reaches Mayorga.
23. 29 December – Moore and Baird unite at Astorga.
24. 29 December – Lord Paget defeats Lefebvre-Desnouettes at Benavente.
25. 29 December – Napoleon reaches Valderas.
26. 30 December – Napoleon reaches Castro Gonzalo.
27. 30 December – Soult defeats La Romana's 2nd Division at Mansilla and La Romana retires.
28. 31 December – Napoleon reaches Benavente.
29. 1 January 1809 – Napoleon reaches Astorga from where Moore had withdrawn.

	British
	Spanish
	French under Napoleon's command
	French under Soult's command

0   20 miles
0   25 km

than 250,000 at his disposal. The order to advance was greeted with delight by the British troops: 'better late than never' according to Ker Porter, though (with hindsight) he remarked that they were 'literally a forlorn hope; and all we can do is assert the honour of England, and to sell our lives dearly'.[29]

Sahagun: charge of the 15th Hussars. (Print after J.P. Beadle)

Moore aimed to march towards Valladolid and to unite the British forces in that region, but first sent back to Portugal his heavy baggage and sick. Baird was ordered to march forward from Astorga, though he had been delayed by his recent withdrawal – Leith's Brigade, for example, only caught up later in the campaign. Lord Paget's light cavalry was ordered to join Moore first, by forced marches. On 9 December Thomas Graham returned from a reconnaissance mission with the news that Madrid had fallen, but Moore was committed; as he reported to Castlereagh, he would be 'in Fortune's way': if she smiled, there was yet time to do some good, and if not at least the effort would have been made (even if belatedly) and the army would have done its duty. It was providential that although too late to save Madrid, Moore's advance was able to prevent Napoleon from administering his intended *coup de grâce*.

On 11 December Moore began to advance from Salamanca, Edward Paget and Beresford's brigade marching to Toro, where they were joined by Lord Paget's cavalry from Baird's force; the band of the 7th Hussars played to celebrate the meeting of the Paget brothers, both in command of the advance-guard of their respective armies. The remainder of Moore's army advanced further east, towards Alaejos and Tordesillas, preceded by Charles Stewart's cavalry, which on 12 December surprised and captured a patrol from the French 22me Chasseurs à Cheval at Rueda. They were from the division of General Jean-Baptiste Franceschi-Delonne, which was covering the southernmost flank of Soult's II Corps, and which lay unsupported at Valladolid, entirely unaware of the proximity of the British. Their ignorance was confirmed when on 14 December Moore received a captured despatch from Napoleon's chief-of-staff, Marshal Berthier, to Soult. The officer carrying it had been killed in a scuffle with a Spanish post-master and the document had been bought for 20 dollars by the British intelligence officer John Waters. It informed Soult that 'You can have no English in your front … everything evinces they are in full retreat … The moment, Marshal, you

are sure that the English have retreated, of which there is every presumption, move forward with rapidity. There are no Spaniards who can resist your two divisions.' The despatch also provided Moore with a complete over-view of the French positions, from which he realised that, although the enemy was more numerous than he had thought, Soult's Corps of 15,000 or 16,000 men was dangerously unsupported in the north. Reinforcements (Junot's corps) were marching towards Soult, but the prospect before Moore was that he might be able to overwhelm Soult before they arrived, the more feasible as it was clear that the French believed the British to be in retreat towards Lisbon.

Accordingly, on 15 December Moore switched the direction of his advance from north-east to north. Part of the British cavalry screen pushed on as far as Valladolid, from where Franceschi retired, north to Medina de Rio Seco and towards Soult. There was some minor skirmishing in which some French prisoners were taken, and on 19 November the 18th Hussars raided Valladolid and carried off some £3,000 from the treasury of the Spanish intendant recently appointed by the French. The remainder of Moore's army marched north, the left column crossing the Douro at Zamora and the right column at Toro, concentrating at Mayorga, and being joined by Baird, by 20 December. The immediate strategic situation began to become clearer; from La Romana Moore received intelligence that Soult was in the region of Saladaña and Carrion, with cavalry pushed forward to Sahagun. However, it also became obvious that little help could be expected from La Romana – no matter how willing the commander and his troops, their equipment was so bad than no more than 7,000 or 8,000 of the 22,000 were capable of taking the field. Moore also received another of the badgering, even insulting, letters from Frere, conveyed by Stuart, as well as a pledge of support from the Supreme *Junta*, which appeared to know little of the realities of the situation of their own armies. In effect, Moore was on his own.

Upon the junction with Baird, Moore reorganised his army entirely, perhaps to leaven Baird's newly arrived units with more experienced corps. It now comprised four infantry divisions (under Baird, Hope,

Fraser and Edward Paget), two light brigades, and two cavalry brigades (under Stewart and the far from competent Slade), with Lord Paget as overall cavalry commander. Only five brigades remained unchanged in composition, one of these – James Leith's – presumably because it was still on the march towards the army from Corunna.

Marshal Soult was aware that there were British troops somewhere in his front – on 19 December he wrote to hurry up the promised reinforcements – but he still expected the enemy to concentrate at Valladolid. Soult's two infantry divisions, at Saldaña and Carrion, were covered by the cavalry brigade of General César-Alexandre Debelle (part of Franceschi's division) at Sahagun, which had been there for some two weeks, observing La Romana.

The recently restored bridge over the river Valderaduey, over which Debelle's troops escaped: looking in the direction of Sahagun. The chapel of Nuesta Señora de la Puente is behind the trees. (Ian Fletcher Battlefield Tours)

SAHAGUN

Leading Moore's advance was Paget's redoubtable light cavalry, which reached the village of Melgar de Abaxo, some twelve miles from Sahagun, on 19 December. Knowing of Debelle's presence there, Paget decided to make a rapid strike with Slade's brigade, accompanied by four guns and his own bodyguard of an officer and twelve men of the 7th Hussars (the regiment of which Paget was colonel). His plan was for Slade, the 10th Hussars and two guns to march west of the river Cea and attack the town of Sahagun from that direction, while Paget and the 15th Hussars would move east of the town and intercept the French as they were driven on by Slade. Each of the British regiments mustered perhaps 500 men (although those actually on the field at Sahagun were probably considerably fewer: it was said that the 15th, for example, left more than 100 men at Melgar de Abaxo). The remaining two guns were

to follow Paget, with the brigade's forage carts. Paget's men began twelve-mile march to Sahagun at about 1.00am on 21 December.

By this time, winter had truly tightened its grip, so that the 15th Hussars' *Sahagun Song*, written the following year, made no exaggeration in describing the march as 'over rivers of ice and o'er mountains of snow'. Ker Porter, who knew Russia, described the weather as resembling Siberia, piercingly cold and damp, so that some men could scarcely hold their reins or swords, and many horses lost their footing. A further disadvantage to the operation was the lamentable Slade – described by Paget as 'that damned stupid fellow' – who seems to have

delayed his approach to Sahagun by delivering a long speech which ended with the declaration, 'Blood and slaughter – march!' (In his defence it is possible that Paget arrived at his destination before the time agreed for the attack, 6.30am, so that he came into action even before Slade should have been ready.)

After a march through a snowstorm and lightning, the 15th Hussars came upon the French forward post some distance from Sahagun. The French piquets were charged immediately, two being killed and a handful captured. However, some of the French troops escaped to carry the alarm into Sahagun.

Approaching from the south, Paget turned east before entering Sahagun, to take up a position to intercept the French as they were driven from the town. But with Slade not having arrived, Debelle was able to assemble his command outside the eastern gate of the town; his two regiments were the 8me Dragoons and the ler Provisional Chasseurs à Cheval, the latter commanded by Colonel Tascher, a relative of the Empress Josephine (although he may not have been present in person). Estimates of their strength range from 500 to 800; papers captured with Debelle's baggage suggested the latter figure, though it probably included detachments not on the field of battle. The regiments began to move eastwards, in the direction of the bridge over the river Valderaduey, parallel to the main road from Sahagun to Carrion and Saldaña but separated from it by a deep ditch or dry watercourse, and across land occupied by vineyards. Looking across the fields as they turned eastwards upon the Sahagun–Carrion road itself, the 15th Hussars could just discern Debelle's men in the darkness, but were unable to identify them. The French were similarly uncertain; as they rode east they threw out skirmishers who repeatedly called to the 15th 'Qui vive?' but held their fire even though they received no reply.

It seems as if Debelle hoped to get ahead of his enemies, to intercept them on the road and attack before they could form; but slowed by the snow and vine-stumps found it impossible to outdistance them, so formed into line behind the ditch, in total six deep, the chasseurs in the first line and the dragoons in the second. As soon as formed they began to cheer and their skirmishers opened fire, by now presuming that the 15th Hussars were Spaniards. At this, Paget immediately wheeled the 15th into line – not exactly matching the French position but with each side's left wing overlapping that of the enemy – and charged. The ditch proved no obstacle and the 15th fell upon the French to the battle-cry of 'Emsdorf and Victory' (referring to a regimental triumph in 1760). Some slight carbine fire was delivered by the French first line, but they appear to have awaited the charge at the halt and were thus entirely overthrown. The chasseurs were driven back upon the dragoons in confusion, and the whole formation collapsed. One of the British officers, Alexander Gordon, described how 'The shock was terrible; horses and men were overthrown, and a shriek of terror, intermixed with oaths, groans, and prayers for mercy, issued from the whole extent of their front'. In moments the action devolved into a flight by the French and a pursuit by the 15th, in such gloomy light that it was difficult to identify friend from foe. 'In many places the bodies of the fallen formed a complete mound of men and horses, but very few of our people were hurt', wrote Gordon,[30] even though it was remarked that the 15th's fur

Fusiliers of the Imperial Guard, who were present in the pursuit of Moore. The Fusilier-Grenadier in the foreground wears the loose overall-trousers commonly used on campaign. (Print after Vilain)

busbies were proven to provide much less protection than the rather more substantial head-dress of the French.

The pursuit continued for more than a mile, until the fugitives reached the river Valderaduey. Paget, riding with the 15th's left centre squadron, halted to send a flag of truce to call upon the French to surrender, but they ignored it and took advantage of the respite to get a head start upon the roads to Carrion and Saldaña, so that further pursuit achieved little. By this stage, most of the 15th were scattered, on tired horses, and so rallying them was difficult. (Paget later scolded them for their ardour, leading to lack of discipline, but they responded by cheering him!) The eventual appearance of Slade caused some consternation – it was at first feared that the 10th Hussars might in fact be more Frenchmen – but the 15th finally rallied and rounded up their prisoners. French casualties are uncertain, but their total loss may have been almost 300, including 157 prisoners, although the British claimed to have killed about 20. Debelle had been unhorsed and ridden over, but managed to escape, though two senior French officers were captured, Colonels Dud'Huit of the dragoons and Dugens of the chasseurs. The 15th Hussars suffered 25 casualties, four of whom were mortally wounded; their commanding officer, Colonel Colquhoun Grant, suffered a slight sabre cut to the head.

The action at Sahagun had a different effect upon the two armies. It must have raised the morale of the British, and was described in Moore's

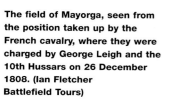

The field of Mayorga, seen from the position taken up by the French cavalry, where they were charged by George Leigh and the 10th Hussars on 26 December 1808. (Ian Fletcher Battlefield Tours)

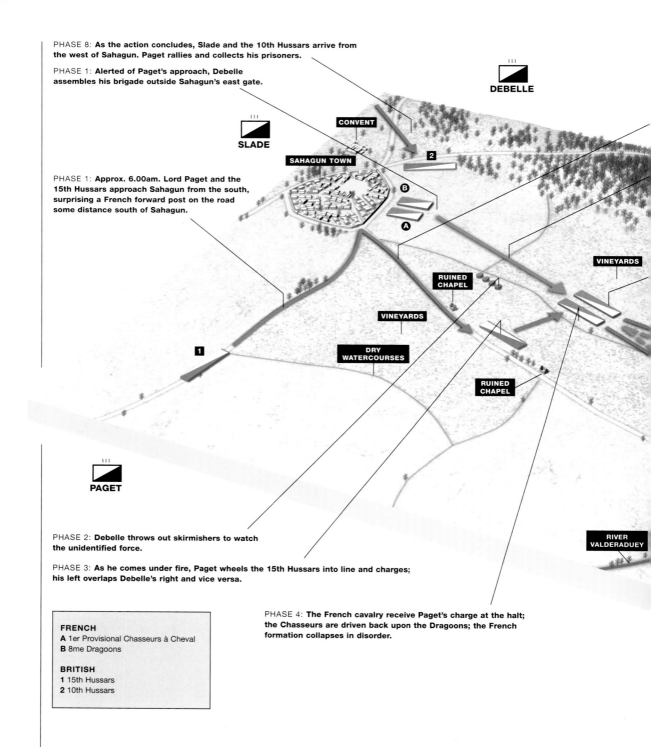

PHASE 8: As the action concludes, Slade and the 10th Hussars arrive from the west of Sahagun. Paget rallies and collects his prisoners.

PHASE 1: Alerted of Paget's approach, Debelle assembles his brigade outside Sahagun's east gate.

PHASE 1: Approx. 6.00am. Lord Paget and the 15th Hussars approach Sahagun from the south, surprising a French forward post on the road some distance south of Sahagun.

DEBELLE

CONVENT

SLADE

2

SAHAGUN TOWN

B

A

VINEYARDS

RUINED CHAPEL

VINEYARDS

DRY WATERCOURSES

RUINED CHAPEL

RIVER VALDERADUEY

PAGET

1

PHASE 2: Debelle throws out skirmishers to watch the unidentified force.

PHASE 3: As he comes under fire, Paget wheels the 15th Hussars into line and charges; his left overlaps Debelle's right and vice versa.

PHASE 4: The French cavalry receive Paget's charge at the halt; the Chasseurs are driven back upon the Dragoons; the French formation collapses in disorder.

FRENCH
A 1er Provisional Chasseurs à Cheval
B 8me Dragoons

BRITISH
1 15th Hussars
2 10th Hussars

THE CAVALRY ACTION AT SAHAGUN

21 December 1808, approx. 6.00am–approx. 7.30am, showing the approach to Sahagun from the south, Lord Paget and the 15th Hussars and their subsequent victorious charge and pursuit.

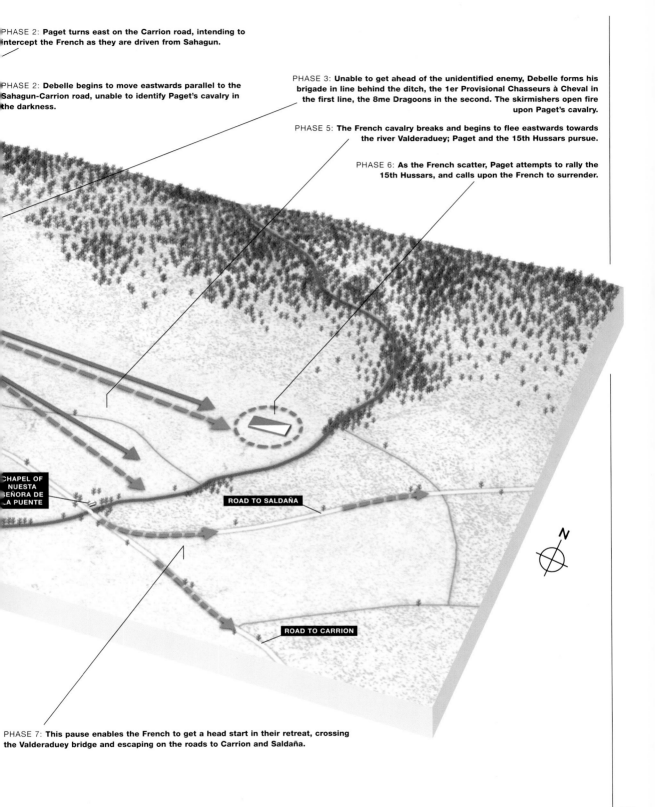

PHASE 2: **Paget turns east on the Carrion road, intending to intercept the French as they are driven from Sahagun.**

PHASE 2: **Debelle begins to move eastwards parallel to the Sahagun-Carrion road, unable to identify Paget's cavalry in the darkness.**

PHASE 3: **Unable to get ahead of the unidentified enemy, Debelle forms his brigade in line behind the ditch, the 1er Provisional Chasseurs à Cheval in the first line, the 8me Dragoons in the second. The skirmishers open fire upon Paget's cavalry.**

PHASE 5: **The French cavalry breaks and begins to flee eastwards towards the river Valderaduey; Paget and the 15th Hussars pursue.**

PHASE 6: **As the French scatter, Paget attempts to rally the 15th Hussars, and calls upon the French to surrender.**

CHAPEL OF NUESTA SEÑORA DE LA PUENTE

ROAD TO SALDAÑA

ROAD TO CARRION

N

PHASE 7: **This pause enables the French to get a head start in their retreat, crossing the Valderaduey bridge and escaping on the roads to Carrion and Saldaña.**

General Order of 22 December as an 'opportunity to display their address and spirit, and assume a superiority which does them credit'; in his journal he described it as 'a handsome thing, and well done'. For Soult, the arrival of the French fugitives confirmed the unexpected proximity of the British. He concentrated his two divisions (led by Generals Pierre-Hugues-Victoire Merle and Julien-Augustin-Joseph Mermet) around Carrion, and sent couriers to speed up the expected reinforcements; those nearest were the division of General Henri-François Delaborde, from Junot's Corps, and the dragoon division of General Jean-Thomas-Guillaume Lorge from the cavalry reserve. By 23 December these were in the vicinity of Palencia; Franceschi's cavalry was still falling back from Valladolid, and Debelle's Brigade was so mauled after Sahagun the ler Provisional Chasseurs were dissolved in January 1809.

Moore brought up his army in the wake of Paget's cavalry and paused at Sahagun, intending to fall upon Soult in the early morning of 24 December. In this he hoped to be aided by as much of La Romana's army as was capable of action, only some 8,000 men and a single battery, which advanced to Mansilla, only some 18 miles north-west of Sahagun. Hope's Division and Alten's Brigade had actually begun their march at nightfall on 23 December, to attack Soult at dawn, when suddenly their orders were countermanded and they were told to return to Sahagun. The reason was more intelligence from La Romana, which suggested that Napoleon had turned north from Madrid, was crossing the Guadarrama mountains and intended to overwhelm Moore. In one sense, Moore had achieved his objective: he had compelled the French to move against him instead of destroying the remaining Spanish resistance, but as a consequence, as he had predicted, he was going to have to 'run for it'.

Ker Porter recalled how the order to retreat crushed the army's morale: 'Every countenance was changed; the proud glow on their cheeks was lost in a fearful paleness ... the army of England was no more. Its spirit was fled; and what appeared to me a host of heroes [became] men in arms without hope, wish, or energy. In my life I never witnessed such an instantaneously withering effect upon any body of living creatures.'[31] David Robertson of the 92nd confirmed it: whereas 'Every heart beat high with the thought that we were to measure arms with the great Napoleon', on receiving the order to turn back, 'All ranks called out to stop and fight and not to run away.'[32]

NAPOLEON'S PURSUIT

Due to failings in the gathering of intelligence, Napoleon had no real idea of the position of the British until late on 19 December, and not until 21 December was he certain enough of Moore's manoeuvres to commit himself fully. Deciding to pause in all his operations against the Spanish, he chose to march every available unit towards the British, whom he presumed to be in the vicinity of Valladolid. Napoleon's reserve from around Madrid got on the march rapidly, including the Imperial Guard, Ney's Corps, most of the reserve division of General Jean-Joseph Dessolle, the division of General Pierre Lapisse from Victor's Corps, and the dragoon division of General Armand Lahoussaye. He ordered Lorge and as much of Junot's Corps as had come up to place themselves under Soult's command, intending Soult to hold Moore's front until he marched up to fall upon the British flank. By turning upon Moore with at least 80,000 men, Napoleon left only enough troops in the vicinity of Madrid to hold the Spaniards in check, not to pursue an offensive; it confirmed Moore's success in buying time to permit the Spanish to rally, but it placed the British in great danger.

Ney's Corps led the advance through the Guadarrama pass on the night of 21 December, arriving at Villa Castin, at the northern end, on the following morning. Napoleon, following with the Imperial Guard, had a much more difficult crossing, as a furious blizzard descended. Even Napoleon had to struggle through the pass on foot; conditions were so bad that Jean-Roch Coignet of the Guard recalled that they were unable to see for the driving sleet and had to hold on to one another to avoid being blown over, but still some men were lost. Aymar de Gonneville, an officer present during the crossing, described how the men of Lapisse's Division 'gave loud expression to the most sinister designs against the Emperor's person, stirring up each other to fire a shot at him, and bandying accusations of cowardice for not doing it. He heard it all as plainly as we did, and seemed as if he did not care a bit for it.'[33] Once through these appalling conditions, however, after food and a rest, the following day the same men cheered Napoleon as he passed!

As Napoleon pushed on in the direction of Benavente (it became clear that Moore was not at Valladolid after all), he expected to trap Moore between himself and Soult. To the latter he wrote that if the British held their position, they would be trapped, but that if they attacked, Soult was to retreat for a day and draw them further into the trap, for 'the farther they proceed, the better for us'. To his brother Joseph at Madrid, Napoleon wrote to say that he would reach Medina de Rio Seco that day (27 December), 'and either today or tomorrow great events will probably take place. If the English have not already retreated, they are lost; and if they retire, they will be pursued so vigorously to their ships, that half of them will never re-embark ... Put into the newspapers, and spread in every direction, that 36,000 English are surrounded, that I am ... upon their rear, whilst Marshal Soult is in front of them.'[34] His triumphal tone was premature, for by that date Moore was well on his way.

21 W. Napier., Vol.I p.422
22 Gardyne, C.G., *The Life of a Regiment*, London 1929, Vol.I p.143
23 Ker Porter, p.168
24 James Moore, p.114
25 Londonderry, pp.179, 181
26 W. Napier, Vol.I p.438
27 ibid., Vol.I p.lxv
28 *United Service Magazine* 1843, Vol.I p.576
29 Ker Porter, pp.193, 196
30 Gordon, p.102
31 Ker Porter, p.235
32 Robertson, p.52
33 De Gonneville, Vol.I p.190
34 Napoleon, Vol.1 p. 387.

SAHAGUN, 21 DECEMBER 1808

Lord Paget's charge with the 15th Hussars at Sahagun was executed with such a fury, despite the difficult nature of the terrain, that the French first line of the 1er Provisional Chasseurs à Cheval was swept away, and driven back upon the second line of the 8me Dragoons. Having overlapped the French line, Paget's left squadron (which had been intended to act as a reserve) originally had no enemy in their front, so the massed ranks of their charge encountered an enemy already reeling, as shown here with the 15th galloping into an already disordered part of the Dragoons. The French were driven towards the river Valderaduey, 'pell mell, cutting and slashing each other' as Alexander Gordon of the 15th recorded, before the British began to rally. The French chasseurs escaped on the road to Carrion, the dragoons by the road to Saldaña. (Christa Hook)

THE RETREAT TO CORUNNA

SAHAGUN TO BENAVENTE

On 24 December Moore began to withdraw, initially only to the mountains beyond Astorga, unless pressed by the French – he still hoped to engage Soult before Napoleon arrived. Two columns marched from Sahagun, Baird's Division taking the northerly route to Astorga via Valencia de Don Juan, Hope and Fraser the southerly route via Mayorga, Castro Gonzalo and the bridge over the river Esla. Edward Paget's Reserve Division, the two light brigades and Lord Paget's cavalry remained a further day at Sahagun to act as a rearguard, the cavalry engaging Soult's forward positions to keep him uncertain about British intentions, involving numerous small skirmishes in which a number of French prisoners were taken. Moore requested that La Romana hold the northerly crossing over the Esla at Mansilla for as long as practicable, and then retire north into the Asturias, leaving Galicia clear for his own retreat.

On Christmas Day Edward Paget's rearguard began to withdraw, taking the southerly route in the wake of Hope and Fraser, with the excellent 3rd Hussars of the King's German Legion providing the last rearguard. On the following day Baird crossed the Esla (with some difficulty) at Valencia de Don Juan, while on the southern route, Ney's advance-guard cavalry pushed on to Mayorga, where they encountered

The castle at Benavente, ransacked by the British on their retreat. (Print after Robert Ker Porter)

General Charles Lefebvre-Desnouettes (1773–1822), commander of the cavalry of the Imperial Guard engaged at Benavente. Taken prisoner during the action, in 1812 he broke his parole, escaped from Cheltenham where he was living, and rejoined Napoleon's army.

Paget's light cavalry rearguard. Soult advanced on the 27th, sending Lorges' dragoons after the British towards Mayorga, while he marched on Astorga, via Mansilla, with the rest. Still without clear intelligence of Moore's location, Napoleon hoped to trap the British between himself and Soult – but Moore was just out of reach. The campaign continued to be a trial against the elements, for a thaw had set in on 24 December, turning roads into mud, sometimes knee deep, further exhausting men already tired by forced marches, so that both Moore and Napoleon lost many men who fell out by the roadside.

For two days Paget's cavalry was involved in running skirmishes with the French advance-guard, against considerable odds and with such success that Napoleon estimated their numbers to be about twice the 2,400 men who were actually present. On 26 December two French squadrons, evidently from the 15me Chasseurs à Cheval of Ney's Corps, captured some men of the 15th Hussars at Mayorga, where the regimental baggage was preceding the retreat. The prisoners were liberated with the help of the 3rd KGL Hussars, but when Lord Paget arrived with the main body he found the French still in Mayorga. They fired at him through the gateway and then withdrew to higher ground. Paget ordered Slade to attack with a squadron of 10th Hussars, but that general hesitated so long (ostensibly to adjust his stirrups) that Paget instructed Colonel George Leigh of the 10th to lead instead. He led one squadron uphill (with another in support), through French carbine fire, halted to re-form, then charged, dispersed the chasseurs and took some 100 prisoners.

Craufurd's Light Brigade covered the southernmost crossing of the Esla at Castro Gonzalo until the last elements of the army had passed. Two privates of the 43rd were posted as sentries, John Walton and Richard Jackson, to warn of the approach of the French advance-guard. When this appeared, as ordered Jackson ran back to raise the alarm, despite suffering 12 or 14 sabre cuts, while Walton defied the cavalry and actually beat them off, emerging unhurt despite having his clothing and equipment cut in more than 20 places, and his bayonet bent double and notched like a saw. Following their sharp reception, the French declined to engage, but Craufurd's men stood in formation, with arms ported, in rain so torrential that Benjamin Harris of the 95th recalled that it actually flowed out of the muzzles of their rifles. Once Paget's cavalry had crossed the river, two arches of the bridge were blown (with a 'tremendous report' according to Harris, which set fire to a nearby house).

Benavente

On 29 December three of Moore's divisions converged at Astorga, Baird from the north, Hope and Fraser from the south, leaving just Paget's reserve and the cavalry on the west bank of the Esla, around the town of Benavente. There was a fine castle at that place, which was ransacked by British troops billeted there overnight; Ker Porter thought the destruction was partly revenge for a perceived lack of assistance from the Spanish, and a belief that they had been lured into their plight by unfulfilled promises, so that the soldiers' indignation was vented upon furniture instead of upon heads! The infantry rearguard marched to Astorga that morning, leaving just the cavalry at Benavente, with picquets along the river. Along the east bank of the Esla was part of the cavalry of the Imperial Guard, the vanguard of Napoleon's force.

Marshal Bessières, commander of the reserve cavalry, was not personally leading the vanguard; instead, its commander was General Charles Lefebvre-Desnouettes, colonel of the Chasseurs à Cheval of the Guard and an officer of noted distinction. Although under orders not to risk his regiment, seeing that he was opposed by only a few British troops, he found a ford and crossed the river with three squadrons of his chasseurs and a small detachment of Mamelukes, in all about 550 men. They drove back the outnumbered British picquets, and beat off a counter-attack by some 130 men commanded by Colonel Loftus Otway of the 18th Hussars. Despite the arrival of some of the German Legion hussars, the confused mêlée of charge and counter-charge led to the British being pushed back some two miles from the river, to the suburbs of Benavente. Charles Stewart rallied them again, and stood to receive what Lefebvre-Desnouettes doubtless intended to be the decisive charge; but from the cover of the suburbs Lord Paget charged the French left flank with the 10th Hussars, which with great skill he had brought up for just such a manoeuvre.

Seeing himself outnumbered, Lefebvre-Desnouettes attempted to withdraw to the ford, but despite his chasseurs making a good effort in a running fight, they were finally broken. Those who reached the river were able to cross it (the French said that some of their men were even rescued from drowning by their British pursuers), but a number were captured. When the French re-crossed the Esla they wheeled about and began to exchange carbine fire with their pursuers, but though reinforced by more French cavalry, they were discouraged from attempting a second crossing when three guns from Downman's troop came up and fired a couple of rounds.

The exact number of casualties in this action is uncertain. Paget's report claimed that the French suffered 30 killed, 25 wounded and 70 prisoners, but other accounts state 9 killed, 98 wounded and

LEFT **The old bridge over the Esla, seen from the 'British' side of the river, successfully blown while Robert Craufurd's brigade discouraged a French attack. (Ian Fletcher Battlefield Tours)**

BELOW **The last surviving part of the castle at Benavente. (Ian Fletcher Battlefield Tours)**

42 captured. Among the latter was Lefebvre-Desnouettes, whose horse was wounded and could not be forced into the water. His capture was credited to Private Levi Grisdale of the 10th Hussars, who as a result became a regimental hero, although it was claimed that Private Johann Bergmann of the German Legion was the one who first accepted the general's surrender, but then rode on to renew the fight, leaving Grisdale with the prisoner. (Although 'Brave on all occasions' Bergmann was described as 'an extremely simple fellow, without any sort of boasting',[35] and so at the time never bothered to claim any credit!) British casualties were about 60, of whom 46 were from the German Legion hussars, including three killed.

ASTORGA TO CACABELLOS

The action at Benavente may have raised the morale of the cavalry, but the decision to continue retreating without having tested the French in battle was a severe blow to the remainder, exacerbated by the rigours of the march and the appalling weather. Already discipline had begun to break down, with troops beginning to pillage for food and plunder. The

47

RIGHT **Benavente: the river Esla viewed from the 'French' side, looking towards the area of the cavalry action of 29 December 1808. (Ian Fletcher Battlefield Tours)**

BELOW **The charge of the 10th Hussars at Benavente, upon Lefebvre-Desnouettes' flank: a later interpretation of the action, first exhibited in 1911. (Print after W.B. Wollen)**

BOTTOM RIGHT
A near-contemporary version of the action at Benavente, showing the 10th Hussars pursuing the Chasseurs à Cheval of the Imperial Guard to the banks of the Esla. The central incident presumably represents the capture of Lefebvre-Desnouettes, although his uniform is not rendered accurately. (Painting by Denis Dighton: The Royal Collection © 2000 Her Majesty Queen Elizabeth II)

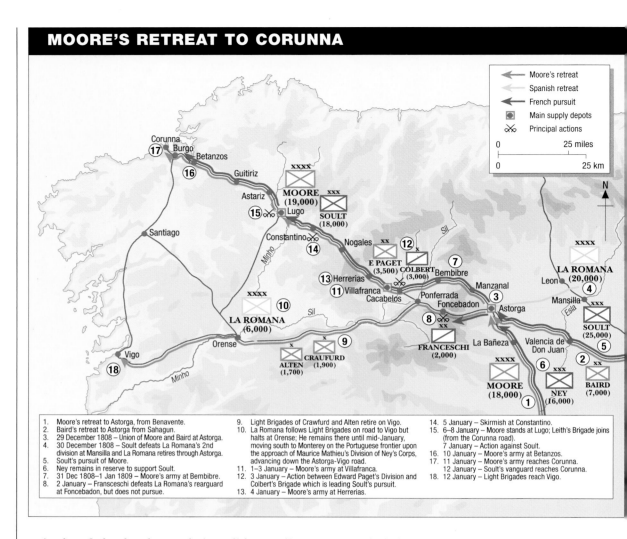

1. Moore's retreat to Astorga, from Benavente.
2. Baird's retreat to Astorga from Sahagun.
3. 29 December 1808 – Union of Moore and Baird at Astorga.
4. 30 December 1808 – Soult defeats La Romana's 2nd division at Mansilla and La Romana retires through Astorga.
5. Soult's pursuit of Moore.
6. Ney remains in reserve to support Soult.
7. 31 Dec 1808–1 Jan 1809 – Moore's army at Bembibre.
8. 2 January – Fransceschi defeats La Romana's rearguard at Foncebadon, but does not pursue.
9. Light Brigades of Crawfurd and Alten retire on Vigo.
10. La Romana follows Light Brigades on road to Vigo but halts at Orense; He remains there until mid-January, moving south to Monterey on the Portuguese frontier upon the approach of Maurice Mathieu's Division of Ney's Corps, advancing down the Astorga-Vigo road.
11. 1–3 January – Moore's army at Villafranca.
12. 3 January – Action between Edward Paget's Division and Colbert's Brigade which is leading Soult's pursuit.
13. 4 January – Moore's army at Herrerias.
14. 5 January – Skirmish at Constantino.
15. 6–8 January – Moore stands at Lugo; Leith's Brigade joins (from the Corunna road).
   7 January – Action against Soult.
16. 10 January – Moore's army at Betanzos.
17. 11 January – Moore's army reaches Corunna.
   12 January – Soult's vanguard reaches Corunna.
18. 12 January – Light Brigades reach Vigo.

attitude of the local population did not discourage such behaviour. Charles Stewart claimed that the Spanish 'met our requisitions for food and wine with murmurs and complaints [which] not unnaturally increased the irritation under which the troops already laboured. They began to view the Spaniards as their worst enemies, and to treat them as people unworthy of any consideration whatever. This was severely retaliated upon them by an enraged peasantry; and scenes of violence and bloodshed, in which these allies were the actors, proved by no means uncommon.'[36] (The withholding of supplies by the civilians is understandable; as was remarked to commissary August Schaumann, they expected the French to follow and would have to provide food for them or risk being hanged!)

On 27 December Moore had issued a sternly worded General Order with his personal observations on 'the extreme bad conduct of the troops … the misbehaviour of the troops … exceeds what he could have believed of British soldiers. It is disgraceful to the officers, as it strongly marks their negligence and inattention … He can feel no mercy towards officers who neglect, in times like these, essential duties, or towards soldiers who disgrace their nation, by acts of villainy towards the country

RIGHT **Fording the Esla: an early engraving.**

they are sent to protect.' The situation in which they were placed, continued Moore, demanded 'qualities the most rare and valuable in a military body … not bravery alone, but patience and constancy under fatigue and hardship, obedience to command, sober and orderly conduct, firmness and resolution'. Finally, acknowledging that the decision not to stand and fight was a major cause of bad behaviour, he added a rather extraordinary note: 'It is impossible for the General to explain to his army the motives for the movements he directs … when it is proper to fight a battle he will do it, and he will choose the time and place he thinks most fit: in the meantime he begs the officers and soldiers of the army to attend diligently to discharge their parts, and leave to him and to the general officers the decision of measure which belong to them alone. The army may rest assured that he has nothing more at heart than their honour and that of his country.'

Moore's criticism of the officers may have been justified. George Napier, at the time an ADC, claimed that 'the men were not so much to blame as the officers [many of whom] were more engaged in looking after themselves and their own comforts, and openly murmuring against the commander-in-chief, than in looking after the soldiers and keeping up proper discipline … the great cause of the disorganised state of the troops was mainly owing to the supineness of the general officers … and to the imprudent language they used themselves, and permitted their staff to make use of, when speaking of the retreat and the conduct of it

Chasseurs à Cheval of the Imperial Guard, the troops which crossed the Esla at Benavente and engaged the British rearguard. (Print by Montigneul after Eugene Lami)

Robert 'Black Bob' Craufurd (1764–1812), distinguished in command of one Moore's light brigades, originally as the rearguard and then on the march to Vigo. He led the Light Brigade, later Light Division, with distinction in Wellington's army, until his death at Ciudad Rodrigo in 1812.

by the commander-in-chief',[37] though he omitted Hope, Bentinck, Paget and Hill from these accusations. Whatever the reason, excepting in Paget's rearguard and some elite units, discipline deteriorated increasingly as the retreat progressed.

Ney's vanguard came up to Castro Gonzalo on 30 December, where the damaged bridge caused a delay in the pursuit (Napoleon remarked that undermining and blowing up the arches was 'a barbarous and unusual use of the rights of war … abhorred by everybody'![38]). Napoleon still hoped that Soult might have caught the British at Astorga, but Soult's march had been so impeded by muddy roads that not until 30 December did he reach Mansilla. There Franceschi's cavalry charged and all but destroyed La Romana's 2nd Division, whereupon La Romana evacuated Leon and, with the route to the Asturias impassable with snow, retired towards Moore at Astorga. The appearance of his army astounded Moore's troops; army doctor Adam Neale saw them stagger in, exhausted, destitute and ravaged by fever, so that he described them as more resembling spectres leaving hospital than an army. Charles Cadell of the 28th remarked, probably with some accuracy, that they were in such an appalling state that 'instead of being any assistance to us, [they] impeded the retreat of the British army, and exhausted the few resources that were left in this unfortunate country. Every house that we entered to shelter us from the inclemency of the weather was filled by those miserable beings, quite destitute of clothing and food.'[39]

Despite the state of his army, La Romana proposed to Moore that they make a stand behind Astorga, blocking the two principal roads to the coast, to Corunna and Vigo, which would also have protected Moore's supply depot at Villafranca and the Spanish artillery park at Ponferrada. Moore declined, partly because he had only two days' food at Astorga and also because he would have had great difficulty bringing more from Villafranca: never adequate, his transport system was breaking down completely from the death from fatigue of the draft animals and the desertion of the local civilian drivers. Although the Astorga position was quite strong, the numerical odds were too great, and Moore probably thought that he had already done what he could in diverting Napoleon's attention from Madrid and from crushing the Spanish armies. (From the content of his correspondence to Castlereagh at this time, however, it is possible that he did not realise how successful he had been, but concentrated all his efforts into saving his army.)

Moore lost no time in ordering the retreat to continue from Astorga, the stores there being distributed to the troops (new muskets to La Romana's army, for example) or destroyed. Even some 400 of the army's sick, too ill to be moved, had to be abandoned. The continuing retreat, in appalling weather, over difficult terrain and with shortages of supplies, exerted an increasing effect upon the army's discipline as marauding, pillage and drunkenness became endemic. Paget's rearguard suffered few such problems, due partly to the character of their commander and partly from the knowledge that they might have to fight at any moment; but other units became mobs of stragglers, stumbling, often barefoot and starving, through mountain passes in the depth of a severe winter. (In places the terrain was extremely hazardous: even Thomas Graham fell over a precipice and had to be rescued by lowering a sash on the end of a sergeant's spontoon for him to climb up!)

OPPOSITE **The pass of Manzanal, between Astorga and Bembibre, illustrating the type of terrain through which Moore's army had to retreat. (Print after Rev. William Bradford)**

By the last day of 1808, Moore's army was clear of Astorga, marching on the high road through the mountains to Corunna. La Romana's army retired due west, on the road to Foncebadon, which led ultimately to the port of Vigo, where the British fleet had been told to wait (until subsequently directed to Corunna). For some time Moore seems to have been uncertain of his destination, and to have been considering turning off the Corunna road and making for Vigo instead. Presumably to keep open this option, he detached both his light brigades just through Astorga, with orders to march to Vigo.

Their march, over rugged and frozen terrain, became a trial of the greatest intensity, although it was only the road and the elements against which they had to battle: they were not pursued by the French. That they reached Vigo in some order, and not as a mob of stragglers, was due in part to the quality of the troops and partly to their leadership. The efforts of the brigade commander, Robert 'Black Bob' Craufurd, to drive on his men and to keep them together have almost passed into legend, and are celebrated in eye-witness accounts like that of Benjamin Harris of the 95th. Unusually for so harsh a disciplinarian, Craufurd was admired and trusted by his men, and Harris had no doubt about his role in saving his command: 'No man but one formed of stuff like General Craufurd could have saved the brigade from perishing altogether; and, if he flogged two, he saved hundreds from death by his management … He seemed an iron man; nothing daunted him – nothing turned him from his purpose. War was his very element, and toil and danger seemed to call forth only an increasing determination to surmount them … I shall never forget Craufurd if I live to a hundred years I think. He was in

Edward Paget (1775–1849), the splendid commander of Moore's rearguard during the retreat to Corunna. Later in 1809 he lost an arm at the passage of the Douro.

THE RETREAT TO CORUNNA AND VIGO

The Retreat to Corunna and Vigo was one of the worst prolonged trials endured by the British army in the Peninsula, conducted over mountainous terrain, in bitter winter weather and in a ragged and shoeless condition. The rearguard held off the French pursuit and maintained its discipline despite the chaos widespread elsewhere on the retreat. That the light brigades held together during their forced march was due to a considerable extent to one of their commanders, 'Black Bob' Craufurd, whose iron discipline and personal example was an inspiration, especially when he would dismount and march on foot, 'that the men might see he took an equal share in the toils which they were enduring' as Benjamin Harris observed. He was, said Harris, 'the very picture of a warrior ... apparently created for command during such dreadful scenes'. (Christa Hook)

Thomas Plunket of the 95th shoots General Auguste de Colbert at Cacabellos. The prone position was one recommended for rifle-shooting. (Print after Harry Payne)

everything a soldier'.[40] Harris remarked that many times Craufurd stopped to harangue parties of exhausted, shoeless soldiers who would stare at him sullenly; and then, as he rode off, they would shoulder their rifles and trudge after him. The two light brigades staggered on until they reached Vigo on 12 January, when the sight of the sea revived their spirits: as William Surtees recalled, 'Fellows without a shoe or a stocking, and who before were shuffling along with sore and lacerated feet like so many lame ducks, now made an attempt to dance for joy'[41] as jokes and laughter replaced the gloomy silence of the previous days.

By depriving the army of two of his best brigades to keep open the possibility of retiring on Vigo, Moore placed the responsibility of maintaining the rearguard upon Edward Paget's Division, plus the 15th Hussars (the terrain being largely unsuitable for cavalry, the others were sent forward to the head of the retreating column). They were followed by the French, but once Napoleon realised that Moore had

The Cua at Cacabellos, near to the location of Plunket's feat of marksmanship. (Ian Fletcher Battlefield Tours)

The retreat: the inhospitable nature of the terrain over which Moore's army had to snake its way is dramatically depicted in this scene. (Print after Robert Ker Porter)

escaped his trap, the urgency declined. Nevertheless, he pressed on, reaching Astorga on 1 January 1809, but had already decided that the task of pursuit did not require all his resources. He ordered Dessolle's Division back to Madrid, then the Imperial Guard, and Lapisse's Division, which had reached Benavente, was ordered to remain there as a 'corps of observation' to pacify the region. On the same day it was said that Napoleon received despatches from Paris which hinted at conspiracies at home. These, and concern over the prospect of war with Austria (which he mentioned in a letter to Joseph from Valladolid on 7 January), decided him to leave the remainder of the campaign in the hands of his subordinates, and he prepared to return to France.

Henceforth, it was Soult who was given the task of hounding Moore, with an increased force. Junot's Corps was broken up, some of its units being sent to join their parent regiments already in Spain, while the divisions of Generals Henri-François Delaborde and Etienne Heudelet were added to Soult's Corps, giving him an effective total of about 25,000 men. The two divisions of Ney's Corps (those of Generals David-Maurice Mathieu de Saint-Maurice and Jean-Gabriel Marchand), some 16,000 men, remained in reserve as a support for Soult, should it be needed, although Ney's cavalry brigade pushed on in the van of the pursuit. It was commanded by one of the most outstanding French cavalry generals, Auguste-François-Marie de Colbert, described by Lejeune as among 'the flower of the army on account of his fine figure, his courteous bearing, and his chivalrous courage'.[42] Soult's vanguard comprised this brigade and Lahoussaye's dragoons, with Merle's Division; Delaborde and Mermet followed, with Heudelet as the rearguard. Franceschi's cavalry was detached towards Foncebadon,

57

where on 2 January they routed La Romana's rearguard, taking about 1,500 prisoners; even Napoleon was shocked by their appearance, telling Joseph that the Spaniards were in 'a horrible state'. Most of the actions which occurred during the pursuit of Moore were carried out by the French cavalry, though several witnesses recorded how they were equipped with enhanced firepower by the practice of mounting a *voltigeur* behind the saddle of some of the dragoons, so that some infantry were usually in the French vanguard.

As the French remarked, even had there been more than one main road through the mountains to Corunna, the course of Moore's retreat was obvious from the wreckage left behind. The difficult road and the weather – Ker Porter called it 'a trackless eternity of winter' – proved too much for many of the draught animals, so the baggage wagons were abandoned along the route, as were many of the exhausted soldiers and their families, whose plight was especially distressing. The plight of the helpless noncombatants can only be imagined. Ker Porter recalled that it was 'truly pitiable to see the trains of women burthened with poor helpless infants, either tied on their backs, or stuffed into the panniers of asses, trudging along, exposed to cold and wet, and all the terrible accidents attending their unassisted situation'.[43] Many accounts exist of women and children collapsing by the road, dying of cold or fatigue, though the resilience of some was remarkable. A number of witnesses of these agonising scenes recorded how several of the soldiers' wives were delivered of children along the road, some of whom perished; but others struggled on with their new-born infants and reached safety. (The wife of Sergeant Monday, the 28th's orderly-room clerk, marched through the entire retreat, and arrived home safely, carrying her lap-dog in a basket over her arm!)

The conditions endured by the soldiers were equally dreadful, as described by Sergeant David Robertson of the 92nd: 'our clothes were

falling off our backs, and our shoes worn to the welts. From the officer down to the private, we were overrun with vermin, bearing alike the extremities of hunger and cold, and forming altogether a combination of suffering sufficient to appall the stoutest heart, and break down the strongest constitution'.[44] The breakdown of discipline intensified under such conditions, and although John Colborne attributed much of the misbehaviour to the minority of 'bad characters' in every regiment rather than to wilful neglect of duty by the majority, hunger compelled some men to stray, to look for food; as one member of the 42nd wrote, 'those that won't fight for their victuals won't fight for their king'![45] As Schaumann remarked, under such trials the laws of war and morality took second place to sheer self-preservation.

As the retreat progressed, order broke down completely; several witnesses recorded 'battalions' consisting of two sergeants bearing the Colours and about thirty men, or as Robertson observed, 'What might now be called the regiment, consisted of the Commanding Officer, the Colours, and about twenty men to act as a guard ... the men were so lame that they could scarcely creep along the road.'[46] The 42nd man remarked that 'I have not language to express what hardships I endured; and if I were to tell you all the men said of this retreat, you would think I had fabricated libels on the memory of Sir John Moore [and] the ministry at home ... on the retreat to Corunna, I thought a soldier's life the most wretched and miserable situation of any that man could be placed in'.[47] Another added that all along the road the trodden snow was just a mass of bloody footprints from the shoeless, lacerated feet of the army.

In his despatch at the end of the retreat Moore stated that 'I could not have believed, had I not witnessed it, that a British army could in so short a time have been so completely disorganized. Its conduct during the late marches has been infamous beyond belief. I can say nothing in its favour but that, when there was a prospect of fighting the enemy, the men were then orderly, and seemed pleased and determined to do their duty.' This was not only reported by the British; one commentator remarked that 'I have heard many French officers assert that ... when all order and discipline appeared to be lost in the British ranks, the slightest prospect of an engagement produced, as if by magic, the immediate restoration of both; the officers, who the moment before appeared wholly without the slightest authority or control, being obeyed upon the instant, as if upon the parade'.[48] The relative quality of leadership was also an important consideration, as exemplified by the 20th's splendid commanding officer, Robert Ross. He was later to achieve great fame during the War of 1812 against the United States from his victory at Bladensburg and death in action while marching to attack Baltimore in 1814. During the retreat to Corunna he insisted that his officers remain with their companies at all times to supervise their men, and it is perhaps no coincidence that although the 20th was continually prepared for action as part of the rearguard, it evidently lost fewer men on the retreat than any other line regiment, bar one.

Charles Steevens (1777–1861); as commander of the 20th's light company, at times during the retreat he led the very last part of Moore's rearguard.

Once through the pass of Manzanal, the army reached Bembibre, where notorious pillaging occurred. There were large supplies of wine in the town, which were broken open as hundreds drank themselves into oblivion. When the rearguard marched in on 1 January 1809 they found the streets full of insensible drunks. Robert Blakeney described the scenes of 'degrading debauchery' as rivers of wine ran in the streets, 'where lay fantastic groups of soldiers … women, children, runaway Spaniards and muleteers, all apparently inanimate … while the wine oozing from their lips and nostrils seemed the effect of gunshot wounds'.[49] All day the rearguard tried to drag them up, but hundreds were incapable even of standing, let alone marching, and had to be left behind. Many were cut up unmercifully by the pursuing French cavalry, but a few escaped and caught up with the army. Moore had them paraded through the ranks to display their hideous mutilations, as a warning of what could happen to those who strayed from their units. Ross was left behind for a short time with his excellent 20th Foot to discourage pursuit, but to his disappointment the French declined to engage formed troops.

The stores depot at Villafranca provided a welcome relief for some (until they arrived there, for example, it was recorded that the 3/1st Royals had received nothing to eat for five days), but the contents of the depot were burned before all had been supplied. There was also a repeat of the scenes of pillage and drunkenness, not even discouraged by Moore having a man shot (albeit probably more for having struck the engineer Captain William Pasley, who was trying to apprehend him, than for plundering). More unconscious drunks had to be left behind when the army moved on (3 January).

Cacabellos

Edward Paget's rearguard was otherwise occupied on 3 January, further back along the road. He halted his five battalions on the high ground behind the bridge over the river Cua at Cacabellos, leaving the 15th Hussars and part of the 1/95th back on the road to Bembibre. A battery of horse artillery was on the western side of the Cua, with the 28th in support, less their light company which was thrown forward to cover the bridge. Paget was trying to discourage plundering by hanging three culprits (whom he pardoned) when in early afternoon the French advance-guard appeared, led by Colbert, who sent for reinforcements to hurry up (Lahoussaye's dragoons and the leading regiment of Merle's division, the 4me *Léger*). Moore himself was present, down from Villafranca, alerted to the French arrival by Slade, who had reported it on behalf of Colonel Grant of the 15th Hussars. Moore asked for how long the general had been Grant's ADC, and stated coldly that Slade's proper place was at the head of his brigade; but he failed to join the 15th for the fight.

Colbert advanced at the head of his brigade, drove back the 15th Hussars and overran the detachment of the 95th, taking 48 prisoners; Moore's secretary, John Colborne, and others of his staff out reconnoitering, had to ride for their lives. The remainder of the outlying British troops crowded over the bridge in some confusion, and Colbert, perhaps not realising the strength of the force before him, attempted to charge after them. Many got across the bridge, but came under heavy cross-fire from the 95th, 52nd and 28th, firing from behind stone walls, and from the artillery. One British participant remarked that 'I never saw men ride more handsomely to destruction', until 'we poured it into them right and left, and they went down like clockwork'.[50] The cavalry was driven back, leaving the road 'absolutely choked with their dead' according to Blakeney of the 28th, and among these was Colbert. He had led the charge but was shot dead by Rifleman Thomas Plunket of the 95th, a noted 'character' and a splendid marksman. (It was said that Plunket had been urged to shoot Colbert by Paget himself, with the promise of a purse of money if he succeeded; though others rejected so base a motive or claimed that it was Thomas Graham who made the offer.) All the British lamented Colbert's fall; as Charles Steevens of the 20th remarked, 'Colonel Ross, and all of us who witnessed it, were very sorry, as he seemed to be a remarkably gallant fellow; but such, alas!, is the fate of war.'[51]

After the retreat of Colbert's Brigade, some of Lahoussaye's dragoons forded the river and began to skirmish with the 52nd and 95th, but when Merle's infantry arrived just before dusk, they came under artillery fire and retired without making much headway. As darkness fell, Moore got his rearguard away without difficulty.

CACABELLOS TO CORUNNA

The retreat continued, with the French hovering around Paget's rearguard, cutting off stragglers. On 5 January, past Nogales, the two carts that were transporting the army's treasury broke down, their bullock teams too exhausted to proceed. The last rearguard, the 28th's flank companies and a company of 95th, stood guard while, as ordered, the casks of dollars were pitched over a precipice rather than let them fall into the hands of the enemy; some £25,000 was disposed of in this way. Some of the money was collected by the pursuing French, more by the local people, and some by British camp-followers: Mrs. Maloney, wife of the 52nd's master-tailor, filled her clothing with coins; she reached Corunna but slipped when boarding her ship, was weighed down by the weight of coins and drowned.

Late on 5 January, at Constantino, the French made another attempt on the rearguard. British engineers having failed to blow up the bridge there, Paget had to cover the river-crossing with artillery, with the banks covered by the 28th and 95th. The French vanguard indulged in some skirmishing, but retired after a few rounds of shrapnel burst over them.

The bridge at Nogales. (Print after Adam Neale)

On 6 January Moore concentrated his army at Lugo, to allow the stragglers to catch up and to give the troops a break from their march (and, as Charles Stewart believed, to offer battle as well). By this time Moore had abandoned the always somewhat impractical plan of retreating to Vigo, had sent orders to the fleet waiting there to sail to Corunna, and now ordered Baird, ahead of him on the road, to halt. He told Baird to send the same orders to Fraser, further ahead still and en route to Santiago, preparatory to marching to Vigo, but Baird sent the message by an orderly from the 15th Hussars who got drunk and never arrived. By the time a second order was sent and Fraser had to counter-march, he had spent two days in unnecessary marching in atrocious weather, and lost 400 men in the process. Moore was 'deeply vexed' at Baird's laxity, but complained little to him; Thomas Graham, however, characteristically made his feelings known. Nevertheless, the main army received supplies from the depot at Lugo, and a welcome reinforcement in Leith's brigade, which finally joined.

Moore issued another stern General Order in expectation of a battle, pleading for a restoration of discipline: 'The Commander of the Forces is tired of giving orders which are never attended to: he therefore appeals to the honour and feeling of the army he commands; and if those are not sufficient to induce them to do their duty, he must despair of succeeding by other means.' He was reported to have declared similar exasperation to the troops directly: 'Soldiers, if you do not behave better, I would rather be a shoe-black than your general.'[52] The prospect of action once again had the effect of assembling the battalions; as Stephen Morley of the 5th Foot remarked, 'sickness, privations, inclement

63

James Leith (1763–1816), commander of the brigade most engaged at Lugo. He became one of the best of Wellington's divisional commanders.

weather, all were alike forgotten: cheerfulness was depicted in every face, alacrity in every movement'.[53] Moore's position was strong, with flanks protected by near-inaccessible terrain, upon rising ground and lined with defensive stone walls, and many expected a battle. Indeed, the eternal enthusiast Thomas Graham asked Moore that once the French had been beaten, 'you will take us in pursuit of them for a few days, won't you?' 'No,' replied Moore, 'I have had enough of Galicia.' 'Oh, just for a few days!' pleaded Graham.[54]

Soult's army came up by degrees, firstly Merle, Lahoussaye and Franceschi, followed by Lorges, Delaborde and Mermet on 7 January; but the effect of forced marches had the same effect upon Soult's army as upon Moore's, with Soult also having stragglers stretched out along the road (Heudelet's division was still only at Villafranca). On the 7th Soult made a tentative movement, notably a demonstration by Merle's Division which was repelled when the 51st and 76th Foot from Leith's Brigade drove back the 2me *Léger* and 36me Line. Even on the following day, when more of his stragglers had caught up, Soult was probably still weaker than Moore (some 18,000 against about 19,000), and he declined to attack, while requesting Ney to push forward to Villafranca. Moore was also wary of attacking, fearing that he would have to face French reinforcements even if he defeated Soult, and on the night of 8 January recommenced his retreat, leaving camp-fires alight to conceal his departure. In the darkness and pouring rain some units became lost and hundreds fell out from fatigue or distress at having retired again without a fight.

Soult was late in realising that Moore had slipped away, and though he sent Franceschi in pursuit, only stragglers were overtaken (some of whom, to their credit, put up some resistance). The French were delayed further by the destruction of the bridge over the river Minho, eight miles north-west of Lugo. On 9–10 January Moore's army staggered into Betanzos, where the rearguard took up a position on high ground outside the town to cover the arrival of thousands of stragglers. Outside the town, a large body of these was attacked by French cavalry. Present there was Sergeant William Newman of the 43rd, who had been left to collect the sick and limping, and he took command of the situation in a quite remarkable manner. He formed up about 100 men across the road, and beat off several attacks, retiring slowly, constantly turning to fire, to allow the rest to get away, and covered the four miles to safety and joined the rearguard. For this heroic action he received an ensigncy in the 1st West India Regiment and a gift of £50, and in 1811 became a lieutenant in the York Light Infantry Volunteers. Nevertheless, about 1,000 men had been lost in the previous two days, some dead of fatigue and exposure but most captured.

Stores had been forwarded to Betanzos to feed the army, and when on 11 January the bulk of it trudged into Corunna the men were in somewhat better heart; the descent from the mountains had brought spring-like weather, and the sight of the sea, as Ker Porter wrote, caused the men to shout as if they had 'beheld a deity'. Much of the army was still disorganised, however, so that the Foot Guards were instantly recognisable at a distance, marching in formation as they had been throughout the retreat, with the drum-major flourishing his staff as if on parade. 'Those must be the Guards,' was Moore's remark as he caught

The commanding nature of Moore's position at Lugo is evident from this view from the 'French' side; the action occurred in the valley between the two positions. (Ian Fletcher Battlefield Tours)

sight of them. Paget's reserve remained behind while engineers endeavoured (with limited success) to blow the bridge at Betanzos. They were interrupted by French cavalry (one courageous sergeant rode on to the middle of the bridge where he was shot by one Thomas Savage of the 28th's light company), and had to pull back. They did, however, succeed in blowing the bridge at El Burgo, four miles from Corunna. When French infantry came up, a day of fairly pointless skirmishing took place across the water, until on 13 January Paget ordered his men to Corunna, upon the arrival of French artillery.

35 Beamish, Vol. 1 p.360
36 Londonderry p.206
37 G. Napier, pp.60–61
38 Napoleon, Vol.I p.388
39 Cadell p.45
40 Harris, pp.92–93, 102
41 Surtees, p.94
42 Lejeune, Vol.I p.115
43 Ker Porter pp.210–11
44 Robertson, p.55
45 Anon., *Forty-Second*, p.61
46 Robertson, p.62
47 Anon., *Forty-Second*, pp.75, 82
48 *United Service Journal* 1840, Vol.III p.32
49 Blakeney, p.50
50 *United Service Magazine* 1843, Vol.I p.577
51 Steevens, p.63
52 *United Service Magazine* 1843, Vol.I p.576
53 Morley, pp.61–62
54 Moore Smith, p.100

THE BATTLE OF CORUNNA

The fleet's passage from Vigo having been delayed by contrary winds, there were insufficient ships in the harbour to evacuate the army as Moore had intended. While waiting, Moore embarked some of his sick and stores into the ships which were there, and re-equipped some 5,000 of his troops with new muskets from the stores which had been landed at Corunna for his use and for that of the Galician *Junta*. The remaining munitions – almost 12,000 barrels of powder and 300,000 musket cartridges, stored in two magazines – were destroyed to deny their use to the French, the explosion of the main magazine on 14 January being so enormous that it caused some structural damage to the city. More than 50 heavy guns from the defences of Corunna were spiked and their carriages thrown into the sea, and with the assistance of Royal Marines landed from the fleet, on 15 January twenty mortars were treated similarly. The inhabitants of Corunna were zealous in working to strengthen the city's defences; Ker Porter remarked that if all Spain had been as courageous and resolute as Corunna's citizens, Napoleon would have been chased back over the Pyrenees by that time.

With the French so near, some of Moore's senior officers suggested treating for an armistice to permit an unhindered evacuation; Moore

RIGHT **The church at Elviña, one of the focal points of the Battle of Corunna. (Ian Fletcher Battlefield Tours)**

The city and harbour of Corunna, seen from the road that approached it.

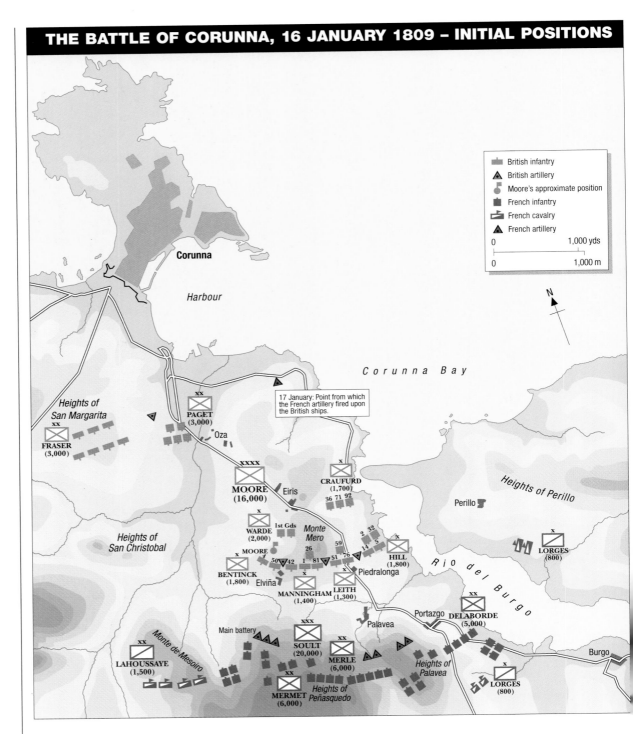

Corunna

Harbour

Corunna Bay

Legend:
- British infantry
- British artillery
- Moore's approximate position
- French infantry
- French cavalry
- French artillery

0   1,000 yds
0   1,000 m

N

Heights of San Margarita

FRASER (3,000)

PAGET (3,000)

Oza

17 January: Point from which the French artillery fired upon the British ships.

CRAUFURD (1,700)

36 71 92

MOORE (16,000)

Eiris

Heights of Perillo

Perillo

WARDE (2,000)

1st Gds

Monte Mero

Heights of San Christobal

MOORE

26

2 32

BENTINCK (1,800)

50 42 1 81 51 76 14 5

59

HILL (1,800)

LORGES (800)

Elviña

MANNINGHAM (1,400)

LEITH (1,300)

Piedralonga

Rio del Burgo

Main battery

SOULT (20,000)

Palavea

Portazgo

DELABORDE (5,000)

Burgo

LAHOUSSAYE (1,500)

Monte de Mesoiro

MERMET (6,000)

Heights of Peñasquedo

MERLE (6,000)

Heights of Palavea

LORGES (800)

rejected this, though when writing to Castlereagh on 13 January he emphasised that he would accept no terms that were in any way dishonourable. This despatch (carried by Charles Stewart, who like Lord Paget was temporarily unfit for service by reason of ophthalmia) was still dismissive of the Spanish military effort, critical of the misbehaviour of his own troops, and ended by remarking that after what had occurred,

The French positions at Corunna, seen from Monte Mero, exemplifying the amount of development which has occurred since 1809. (Ian Fletcher Battlefield Tours)

there would surely be no further intention of sending British troops to Spain.

On 14 January the ships arrived and Moore began to embark, beginning with the artillery and cavalry. Many cavalry horses had been shot as their strength gave out on the march, and those which could not be accommodated aboard ship were destroyed, a traumatic experience for the troops involved. During the retreat the British had lost about 5,000 men, but there still remained ashore at Corunna about 15,000 infantry, a few gunners and a small picquet of 15th Hussars.

Soult approached Corunna slowly. By 14 January the El Burgo bridge had been repaired sufficiently to accommodate his artillery, and thus he moved up the divisions of Mermet and Merle, and the cavalry of Lahoussaye and Lorges. Franceschi's Division, sometimes stated as being involved in the Battle of Corunna, had evidently been sent westwards, to explore the area in the direction of Santiago.

To cover embarkation, Moore selected a defensive position about two miles south of Corunna, centred upon a ridge of high ground, Monte Mero. About a mile to the south it was overlooked by the higher ground of the Heights of Palavea and Peñasquedo, and Monte de Mesoiro; between the two ran the Palavea stream, and the village of Elviña stood on a lower neck of terrain. The Monelos stream ran in a northerly direction, between Monte Mero and the high ground to the west, the Heights of San Cristobal and Santa Margarita. The terrain was unsuitable for cavalry, 'a complete network of walls, hedges, and rows of olive-trees and aloes, of such intricacy that I should imagine it nearly impossible to have formed fifty men abreast anywhere'[55] as Basil Hall recalled.

On 15 January Soult manoeuvered into position on the Peñasquedo and Palavea Heights, and Moore deployed his army to face the French, with Hope's Division on the left and Baird on the right. From the left flank, resting on the estuary, there were deployed Hill's Brigade (from left to right, 5th and 14th Foot, 32nd and 2nd in reserve); Leith's Brigade (76th and 51st, 59th in reserve); Manningham's Brigade

The explosion of the magazines at Corunna. (Print after Robert Ker Porter)

Lord William Henry Cavendish Bentinck (1774–1839); son of the then Prime Minister, the 3rd Duke of Portland, Bentinck led the brigade heavily engaged around Elviña. (Engraving by G. Stodart after Sir Thomas Lawrence)

(81st and 1st, 26th in reserve); and on the slopes above Elviña, Bentinck's Brigade (42nd, 50th and 4th) with Warde's Guards Brigade in reserve. Further back along the estuary was Catlin Craufurd's Brigade (36th, 71st and 92nd). Paget's Division was westward and to the rear, covering the right flank, and Fraser's Division in Corunna. (One of Paget's brigades had lost its commander: Robert Anstruther had died on reaching Corunna, of 'an inflammation of the lungs' brought on by the rigours of the retreat.) All Moore's artillery had been embarked, save Truscott's and Wilmot's companies, and four of their guns were later withdrawn and replaced by Spanish 8-pdrs. Three guns were allocated to Paget and the remainder distributed mainly in pairs along the line.

As Soult deployed there was some skirmishing around Palavea, in which the British advance posts were thrown back, and LtCol John Mackenzie, commander of the 5th Foot, was mortally wounded leading his light company in an unsuccessful attempt to capture two French guns. Later on 15 January Soult was reinforced by the arrival of Delaborde's Division (Heudelet was still far away), and he established a twelve-gun battery on the heights of Peñasquedo opposite Elviña (in all he had about 40 guns). From left to right he deployed Lahoussaye's dragoons, the divisions of Mermet, Merle and Delaborde, with Lorges' dragoons partly on the right flank and partly on the Heights of Perillo, on the opposite side of the estuary. His exact strength is uncertain: French sources suggest 16,000 but other put their numbers as high as 20,000.

Soult intended to make his main thrust with Mermet's Division around Elviña, intending to turn Moore's flank and roll up his line, and perhaps cutting off his line of retreat to Corunna, while the rest of the British line would be kept occupied by Merle and Delaborde. The terrain was so rugged, however, that his deployment was delayed so long on 16 January that Moore presumed there would be no action. In the early afternoon Moore ordered Paget's Division to march to the harbour

The Battle of Corunna. This later engraving shows Moore cheering on the 42nd but the uniforms are not accurate. The building in the background is intended to represent the church at Elviña.

and embark, the remainder to follow at dusk; Moore remarked to Colborne that 'If there is no bungling, I hope we shall get away in a few hours,' but only minutes later Soult began to advance. Paget's men had marched barely 100 yards towards the harbour before the sound of gunfire caused them to halt, while Moore ordered Fraser out of Corunna and to a position to protect the extreme right flank, on the Heights of Santa Margarita.

The first shots had an electrifying effect. The naval officer Basil Hall had toured the British line that morning and found an uncanny silence among the troops, who looked exhausted, and were either asleep or gazing towards the ships. He asked an officer if anything could rouse them: 'You'll see by-and-by, sir, if the French there choose to come over.' At that moment the French artillery opened fire, whereupon 'the whole of the British troops, from one end of the position to the other, started on their feet, snatched up their arms, and formed in line with as much regularity and apparent coolness as if they had been exercising on the parade in Hyde Park. I really could scarcely believe my eyes when I beheld these men spring from the ground, full of life and vigour, though but one minute before they had been stretched out listlessly in the sun. I have already noticed the silence which reigned over the field; now, however, there could be heard a loud hum, and occasionally a jolly shout, and many a peal of laughter, along the distance of nearly a mile. In the midst of these sounds the peculiar sharp "click-click-click" of fixing bayonets fell distinctly on the ear, very ominously … Not a single face could now be seen turning towards the ships … All had become animation and cheerfulness in minds from which, but a short time before, it seemed as if every particle of spirit had fled.'[56] Representative

71

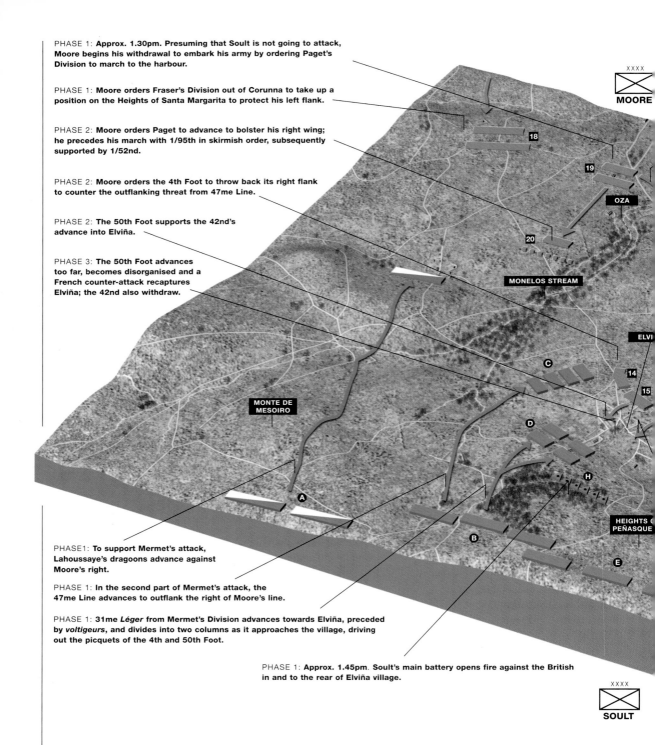

PHASE 1: **Approx. 1.30pm. Presuming that Soult is not going to attack, Moore begins his withdrawal to embark his army by ordering Paget's Division to march to the harbour.**

PHASE 1: **Moore orders Fraser's Division out of Corunna to take up a position on the Heights of Santa Margarita to protect his left flank.**

PHASE 2: **Moore orders Paget to advance to bolster his right wing; he precedes his march with 1/95th in skirmish order, subsequently supported by 1/52nd.**

PHASE 2: **Moore orders the 4th Foot to throw back its right flank to counter the outflanking threat from 47me Line.**

PHASE 2: **The 50th Foot supports the 42nd's advance into Elviña.**

PHASE 3: **The 50th Foot advances too far, becomes disorganised and a French counter-attack recaptures Elviña; the 42nd also withdraw.**

PHASE1: **To support Mermet's attack, Lahoussaye's dragoons advance against Moore's right.**

PHASE 1: **In the second part of Mermet's attack, the 47me Line advances to outflank the right of Moore's line.**

PHASE 1: **31me *Léger* from Mermet's Division advances towards Elviña, preceded by *voltigeurs*, and divides into two columns as it approaches the village, driving out the picquets of the 4th and 50th Foot.**

PHASE 1: **Approx. 1.45pm. Soult's main battery opens fire against the British in and to the rear of Elviña village.**

XXXX
MOORE

XXXX
SOULT

OZA

MONELOS STREAM

MONTE DE MESOIRO

ELVI

HEIGHTS (PEÑASQUE

18   19   20   14   15

A   B   C   D   E   H

THE BATTLE OF CORUNNA, 16 JANUARY 1809

First Stage, from approx. 1.30pm to approx. 3.00pm, showing Moore's attempts to begin embarkation of the army, Soult's opening artillery barrage against the village of Elviña, Mermet's attack and the beginnings of Moore's counter-attack

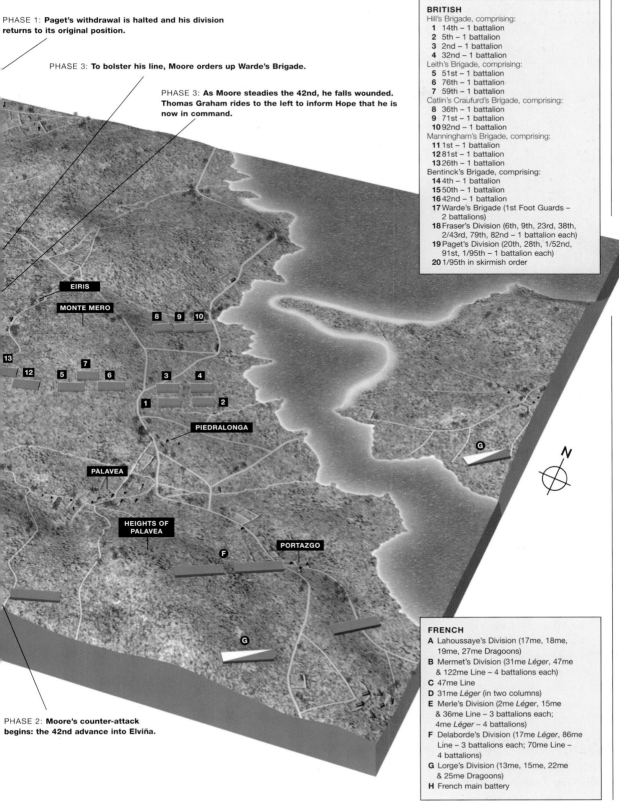

PHASE 1: **Paget's withdrawal is halted and his division returns to its original position.**

PHASE 3: **To bolster his line, Moore orders up Warde's Brigade.**

PHASE 3: **As Moore steadies the 42nd, he falls wounded. Thomas Graham rides to the left to inform Hope that he is now in command.**

PHASE 2: **Moore's counter-attack begins: the 42nd advance into Elviña.**

EIRIS

MONTE MERO

PIEDRALONGA

PÀLAVEA

HEIGHTS OF PALAVEA

PORTAZGO

BRITISH
Hill's Brigade, comprising:
  1 14th – 1 battalion
  2 5th – 1 battalion
  3 2nd – 1 battalion
  4 32nd – 1 battalion
Leith's Brigade, comprising:
  5 51st – 1 battalion
  6 76th – 1 battalion
  7 59th – 1 battalion
Catlin's Craufurd's Brigade, comprising:
  8 36th – 1 battalion
  9 71st – 1 battalion
  10 92nd – 1 battalion
Manningham's Brigade, comprising:
  11 1st – 1 battalion
  12 81st – 1 battalion
  13 26th – 1 battalion
Bentinck's Brigade, comprising:
  14 4th – 1 battalion
  15 50th – 1 battalion
  16 42nd – 1 battalion
  17 Warde's Brigade (1st Foot Guards – 2 battalions)
  18 Fraser's Division (6th, 9th, 23rd, 38th, 2/43rd, 79th, 82nd – 1 battalion each)
  19 Paget's Division (20th, 28th, 1/52nd, 91st, 1/95th – 1 battalion each)
  20 1/95th in skirmish order

FRENCH
A Lahoussaye's Division (17me, 18me, 19me, 27me Dragoons)
B Mermet's Division (31me *Léger*, 47me & 122me Line – 4 battalions each)
C 47me Line
D 31me *Léger* (in two columns)
E Merle's Division (2me *Léger*, 15me & 36me Line – 3 battalions each; 4me *Léger* – 4 battalions)
F Delaborde's Division (17me *Léger*, 86me Line – 3 battalions each; 70me Line – 4 battalions)
G Lorge's Division (13me, 15me, 22me & 25me Dragoons)
H French main battery

ABOVE **The 42nd engaged at Elviña. Executed about a century after the event, this picture is not authentic in its details but is evidence of the enduring interest in the battle. (Print after R. Caton Woodville)**

of the general spirit of the army was an officer of the 32nd so exhausted by the retreat that he was scarcely able to stand, so his men found him an armchair in which he sat during the battle, so as not to miss the fighting!

As Soult's main battery continued to fire, two of Mermet's brigades advanced towards Elviña, led by Generals Joseph-Yves Manigault-Gaulois (who was to be killed in the battle) and Henri-Antoine Jardon. The latter was somewhat of a 'character', known as 'the *voltigeur* general', who marched alongside the ordinary soldiers and was popular with them for his rough manners and unpolished bearing. The French advance-guard drove the picquets of the 4th and 50th Foot from Elviña, and the attack developed into two parts as the main body came on. Towards Elviña, the 3lme *Léger* divided into two columns as it approached the village, while at the left the 47me Line made to outflank the British position. Major Charles Napier, commanding the 50th, quite distinctly heard them shouting 'En avant!' and 'Tue! Tue!'

Napier was talking to Lord William Bentinck (who was mounted on a mule and chatting with the utmost calm) when Moore rode up at speed,

ABOVE, RIGHT **Moore receives his fatal wound: an early but remarkably inaccurate engraving of the scene!**

upon a striking, cream-coloured horse, his expression more intent and his gaze more piercing than Napier had ever seen. He galloped away, then returned and sanctioned the reinforcement of the 50th's skirmishers, so Napier ordered forward his grenadiers, instructing their captain to 'open the ball'. This officer, William Clunes, was a powerful man 6ft 5in tall, and it was presumably at this stage of the battle that he jumped in among a party of six French sharpshooters, striking down or taking prisoner all of them, using only a heavy blackthorn stick which he carried in preference to a sword. All this time, Bentinck's Brigade had been battered by artillery fire, and one shot struck off the leg of a 42nd man, who shrieked and rolled around, clearly upsetting his comrades. Moore called for him to be carried away, adding, 'My good fellow, don't make such a noise; we must bear these things better.'

Moore rode to the right flank and instructed the 4th to throw back their right wing to protect against the intended encircling movement by the 47me; it was executed with such precision that Moore called to the battalion commander, LtCol James Wynch, 'That is exactly how it should be done.' He then returned to Elviña, where it appears that, at Moore's behest, Baird had ordered forward the 42nd to begin the British counter-attack. Baird had then fallen wounded when a roundshot took off his left arm, so Moore himself exhorted the 42nd: 'My brave Highlanders! Remember Egypt!' The battalion had been lying down, but leaped up, cheered, fired at close range and charged the surprised head of the column of the 3lme *Léger*, halting along a wall-line just above the village: 'The confusion that now ensued baffles all my powers even of

THE BATTLE OF CORUNNA

When the British launched their counter to the French attack on the village of Elviña, they had some success, but cohesion was lost in the fighting among the buildings and lanes. Major Charles Napier of the 50th Foot led a small party of his regiment along a lane leading south from the village, charging towards the French position, and towards a barricade built the previous day across the lane. They came under fire from all sides – from their own as well as from the French 31me *Léger* – and the counter-attack was driven back with heavy casualties. Napier himself – who admitted the handicap of being very short-sighted and without his spectacles – was wounded and captured as he tried to rejoin the remainder of his regiment, which was still sheltering in the village. (Christa Hook)

memory and imagination – pell-mell, ding-dong' as one recalled.[57] It was presumably about this time that the three British guns in the position were attacked, two 6-pdrs and one 8-pdr; the latter was overrun, but not before the NCO in command had spiked it, despite being shot six times in the right arm.

Napier of the 50th had received no orders to join the counter-attack, and had his men perform arms drill to occupy their minds against the artillery barrage, and lowered the Colours lest they attracted shot. After an experienced Scottish officer remarked to him that he couldn't be wrong in following the 42nd, Napier ordered the advance against the 3lme *Léger*'s left column. This was driven back in such style by Napier and his deputy, Major Charles Stanhope, that Moore shouted to them, 'Well done 50th! Well done, my majors!' The French were driven from the

village – a detachment which tried to hold the church was captured – but Napier led some of his men onward, into the lanes beyond Elviña. The battalion was broken up by the confused fighting, and only about thirty men followed Napier in an injudicious advance towards the French guns. Under fire from both sides and isolated, Napier tried to call up the remainder of his men, but having taken cover, they were reluctant to move; the more so when Stanhope, trying to lead a charge in support, was shot dead on the spot. Bentinck then appears to have ordered the 50th to withdraw. Unable to obtain reinforcements and in a rage of despair at the thought that his regiment had failed, Napier cast about for help until, with almost all his companions felled or fled, he was shot above the ankle. Engulfed by the French counter-attack which charged back into Elviña, Napier was bayonetted and clubbed, but was twice

Corunna: this early scene of the action evidently is intended to show the advance of the 42nd (left centre), while the French attack from the right. The officers in the left mid-ground are apparently clustered around the injured Moore.

SIR JOHN MOORE AT CORUNNA

As the French attacks pressed on towards Elviña, and attempted to outflank Bentinck's Brigade, Sir John Moore was present to direct the British response. He rode from one battalion to another, eyes always fixed upon the developing fight with a look 'of searching intenseness beyond the power of words to express' according to Charles Napier. Here he is pictured watching the battle while conversing with Lord William Bentinck, who was dismounted from the mule he rode during the action. Behind Moore, his friend Thomas Graham speaks to one of his countrymen, a field officer of the 42nd Highlanders, while members of that regiment's light company rush towards the firing line. It was while he was with the 42nd that Moore received his mortal wound from the French artillery that had been raking the British position. (Christa Hook)

saved by a French drummer named Guibert, who prevented him from being killed, and he was helped away by an old soldier of the 50th, named Hennessy, who had surrendered only with the greatest reluctance. Napier was taken to one of Merle's brigadiers, General Hilaire-Benoît Reynaud, who had his wounds dressed.

With Elviña back in French hands, and the need for the 50th, if not also the 42nd, to reorganise, Moore had a difficult problem. He had only sketchy reports of the attempt to outflank his right – in addition to the advance of the 47me, Lahoussaye's dragoons were advancing on the Heights of San Cristobal – and so far Paget had not appeared in response to Moore's order to advance. He therefore ordered up Baird's divisional reserve, Henry Warde's two splendid battalions of the 1st Foot Guards, to bolster the line and perhaps execute another counter-attack upon Elviña. Their approach, however, seems to have given the impression to the 42nd that they were being relieved and, already short of ammunition, they began to fall back. Seeing the light company retiring, Moore had to check them in person: 'My brave 42nd … you still have your bayonets! Recollect Egypt!'. They returned to the fighting immediately, and Moore doffed his hat to them in thanks. As his aide Henry Hardinge rode up from summoning the Guards, Moore pitched from his saddle. Thomas Graham thought at first that he was unhurt, for Moore made no murmur; but was appalled to see that the general's left arm had been almost severed by a roundshot which had hit his shoulder. Surgeon McGill of the Royals was on hand, and realised at once that the wound was mortal.

Moore never flinched, keeping his eyes upon the battle, though he knew his fate as he told Hardinge, who was trying to staunch the blood with his sash. As Moore was moved his sword-hilt entered the wound, but he stopped Hardinge from unbuckling his belt, remarking that 'It is as well as it is. I had rather it should go out of the field with me.' He was placed in a blanket and carried towards Corunna by men of the 42nd; he sent away the surgeons who had been attending to Baird's injury, remarking that they could not help him, but could assist other wounded men. Wynch of the 4th, also on his way to the rear, wounded, offered Moore the cart in which he was travelling, but the Highlanders assured Moore that they could give him a smoother ride, so continued to bear him to the rear. Graham rode to tell Hope that he was now in command.

The fighting continued in Elviña for some time, as dusk began to fall. Mermet fed in his reserves, and although the reinforced British pushed forward some way, part of the village appears to have remained in French hands until the fighting died down, with darkness and probably mutual exhaustion. Merle tried to support the French in Elviña, advancing his left wing towards the village, but this was countered by Manningham,

ABOVE, LEFT **Charles James Napier (1782–1853), who commanded the 50th Foot at Corunna. He recovered from the injuries he sustained in the battle and rose to the rank of lieutenant-general, winning especial distinction in India. He was a brother of the great historian William Napier.**

Moore is carried from the field; a much later illustration which mistakenly shows the 1812 regulation uniform worn by the British troops. (Print after H. Dupray)

who advanced the 1st and 81st down the slope and engaged the 4me *Léger* in their flank. The French column turned to meet the threat and a fight of some duration ensued, Merle supporting his men with the 2me *Léger*. After the 81st had suffered considerable casualties and had run out of ammunition, Hope replaced them with the reserve of Leith's brigade, the 59th. A further advance by some of Merle's right flank against Leith appears not to have involved any serious fighting, and the French withdrew, leaving some desultory skirmishing to take place.

On the western side of the battle, the attempt to outflank Moore's right was halted by the arrival of Paget's Division, after Wynch's 4th Foot, protected by a ditch and a wall, delayed the advance of the 47me Line. Paget preceded his advance with the 1/95th in skirmish order, subsequently reinforced by the 52nd, with his remaining three battalions in support. The 20th and 91st Foot moved to support Bentinck's right flank, while the others advanced along the valley. The terrain was unsuited for cavalry action, with its gullies and walls, so Lahoussaye was unable to stop the advance, despite the 27me Dragoons being dismounted and deployed as skirmishers. The arrival of Paget's Division forced Mermet to

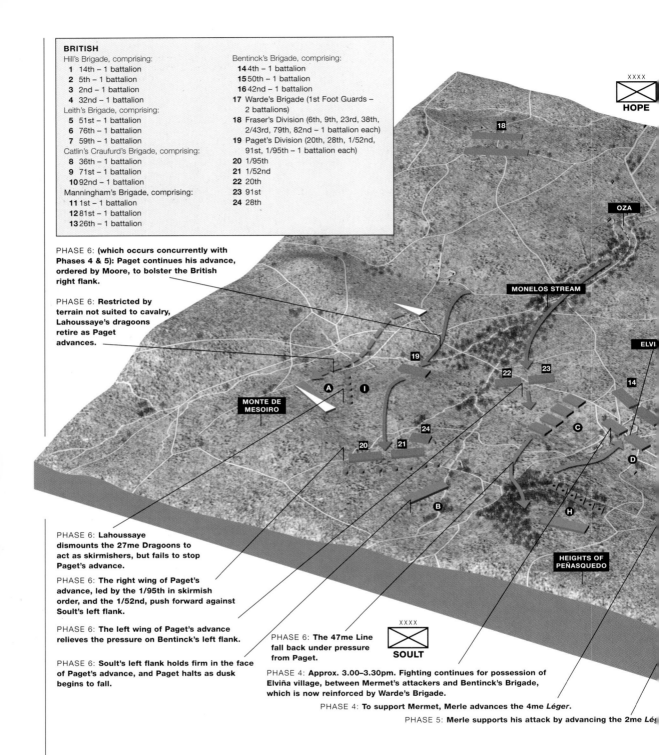

BRITISH

Hill's Brigade, comprising:
1 14th – 1 battalion
2 5th – 1 battalion
3 2nd – 1 battalion
4 32nd – 1 battalion

Leith's Brigade, comprising:
5 51st – 1 battalion
6 76th – 1 battalion
7 59th – 1 battalion

Catlin's Craufurd's Brigade, comprising:
8 36th – 1 battalion
9 71st – 1 battalion
10 92nd – 1 battalion

Manningham's Brigade, comprising:
11 1st – 1 battalion
12 81st – 1 battalion
13 26th – 1 battalion

Bentinck's Brigade, comprising:
14 4th – 1 battalion
15 50th – 1 battalion
16 42nd – 1 battalion
17 Warde's Brigade (1st Foot Guards – 2 battalions)
18 Fraser's Division (6th, 9th, 23rd, 38th, 2/43rd, 79th, 82nd – 1 battalion each)
19 Paget's Division (20th, 28th, 1/52nd, 91st, 1/95th – 1 battalion each)
20 1/95th
21 1/52nd
22 20th
23 91st
24 28th

HOPE

OZA

18

MONELOS STREAM

ELVI

19

22   23

14

MONTE DE MESOIRO

A   I

24

C

20   21

D

B

H

HEIGHTS OF PEÑASQUEDO

SOULT

PHASE 6: (which occurs concurrently with Phases 4 & 5): Paget continues his advance, ordered by Moore, to bolster the British right flank.

PHASE 6: Restricted by terrain not suited to cavalry, Lahoussaye's dragoons retire as Paget advances.

PHASE 6: Lahoussaye dismounts the 27me Dragoons to act as skirmishers, but fails to stop Paget's advance.

PHASE 6: The right wing of Paget's advance, led by the 1/95th in skirmish order, and the 1/52nd, push forward against Soult's left flank.

PHASE 6: The left wing of Paget's advance relieves the pressure on Bentinck's left flank.

PHASE 6: Soult's left flank holds firm in the face of Paget's advance, and Paget halts as dusk begins to fall.

PHASE 6: The 47me Line fall back under pressure from Paget.

PHASE 4: Approx. 3.00–3.30pm. Fighting continues for possession of Elviña village, between Mermet's attackers and Bentinck's Brigade, which is now reinforced by Warde's Brigade.

PHASE 4: To support Mermet, Merle advances the 4me *Léger.*

PHASE 5: Merle supports his attack by advancing the 2me *Lég*

THE BATTLE OF CORUNNA 16 JANUARY 1809

Second Stage, from approx. 3.30pm to approx. 6.00pm
Moore having been wounded, Hope takes command of the British Army. The struggle for Elviña village and the centre of the line continues, while Paget's advance on the British right flank continues

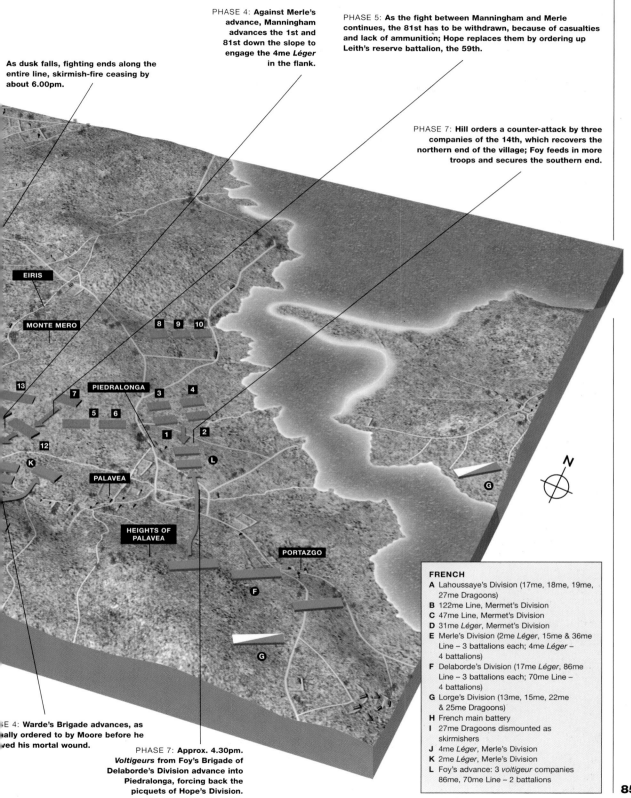

PHASE 4: Against Merle's advance, Manningham advances the 1st and 81st down the slope to engage the 4me *Léger* in the flank.

PHASE 5: As the fight between Manningham and Merle continues, the 81st has to be withdrawn, because of casualties and lack of ammunition; Hope replaces them by ordering up Leith's reserve battalion, the 59th.

As dusk falls, fighting ends along the entire line, skirmish-fire ceasing by about 6.00pm.

PHASE 7: Hill orders a counter-attack by three companies of the 14th, which recovers the northern end of the village; Foy feeds in more troops and secures the southern end.

EIRIS

MONTE MERO

8 9 10

13

7 PIEDRALONGA 3 4

5 6

1 2

12

K L

PALAVEA

HEIGHTS OF PALAVEA

PORTAZGO

F

G

G

N

E 4: Warde's Brigade advances, as ...ally ordered to by Moore before he ...ved his mortal wound.

PHASE 7: Approx. 4.30pm. *Voltigeurs* from Foy's Brigade of Delaborde's Division advance into Piedralonga, forcing back the picquets of Hope's Division.

FRENCH
A Lahoussaye's Division (17me, 18me, 19me, 27me Dragoons)
B 122me Line, Mermet's Division
C 47me Line, Mermet's Division
D 31me *Léger*, Mermet's Division
E Merle's Division (2me *Léger*, 15me & 36me Line – 3 battalions each; 4me *Léger* – 4 battalions)
F Delaborde's Division (17me *Léger*, 86me Line – 3 battalions each; 70me Line – 4 battalions)
G Lorge's Division (13me, 15me, 22me & 25me Dragoons)
H French main battery
I 27me Dragoons dismounted as skirmishers
J 4me *Léger*, Merle's Division
K 2me *Léger*, Merle's Division
L Foy's advance: 3 *voltigeur* companies 86me, 70me Line – 2 battalions

85

Major-General Coote Manningham, whose brigade helped to repel the French attack upon the British centre at Corunna; he is depicted here in the uniform of the 95th Rifles, a corps he helped to establish. He died at Maidstone in August 1809 of illness and fatigue brought on by the rigours of the Corunna campaign.

abandon the attempt to turn Bentinck's flank, and the French turned to meet the new threat. They fell back on their original position, and though it has been claimed that the 95th advanced so far as to threaten the French battery, as dusk fell Paget halted at the foot of the enemy position, which was still held by Mermet's reserves. (One participant claimed that Paget's advance stalled from lack of ammunition; the French, he wrote, 'looked shaky, and I believe very little would have sent them off, for I observed some of them pulling down a stone wall on their right to make an opening. Oh! for a few thousand rounds of ammunition, then!'.[58] The 95th claimed to have taken 7 officers and 156 other ranks prisoner, for the loss of 12 dead and 8 prisoners.

On the extreme east of the battle, it was late afternoon (about 4.30pm) before Delaborde made any serious effort against the British position, *voltigeurs* from the brigade of General Maximilien-Sébastien Foy advancing into the village of Piedralonga. There they pushed back the picquets of Hope's Division (evidently selected from the whole division, as they included members of the 92nd from Craufurd's Brigade, which was otherwise in reserve). Their commander was LtCol Alexander Napier of Blackstone of the 92nd, who was hit in the groin as he prepared a counter-attack; one of his men bound the wound with his shirt, but it proved mortal. Hill ordered forward Colonel Jasper Nicolls with three companies of his 14th Foot which recovered the northern end of the village, but Foy fed in more troops and secured the southern part. David Robertson claimed that fierce fighting ensued – 'such bayonet work I never saw before' – but it can hardly have been so serious. Only about one-third of Foy's Brigade had been engaged (two battalions of the 70me Line, and the three *voltigeur* companies of the 86me), with a loss of only 18 dead and 50 wounded from the 70me and a few from the 86me; the 92nd lost only three dead and five wounded, one of whose injuries proved fatal.

As darkness fell the fighting ended, even skirmish-fire ceasing by 6.00pm, without much territorial advantage to either side: the British had a stronger presence in Elviña than before the battle began, and the French had a foothold in Piedralonga. Some criticised Hope for not pressing the attack on Soult's left flank and for not committing Fraser's Division (Blakeney of the 28th, for example, thought that had Moore been in command he would have been satisfied only with the enemy's total destruction), but such an outcome might not have been inevitable, as a considerable proportion of Soult's army had never been engaged. In any case, Hope would still have had to evacuate his army from Corunna even had Soult been annihilated.

Losses in the battle are difficult to assess. Hope's despatch thought his total casualties 'did not exceed in killed and wounded from seven to eight hundred', though even that may have been over-estimated. Most casualties were concentrated among a few units: evidently the 50th lost five officers and 180 other ranks, the 42nd 39 dead and 111 wounded, the 81st 30 dead and 133 wounded. The units on the flanks suffered much less: the 4th lost 3 killed and 14 wounded and even the two leading units of Paget's Division (1/95th, 52nd) together lost only 17 dead and 66 wounded. Soult's loss seems even more difficult to ascertain: Hope's estimate, that the French suffered nearly double his own loss, may not be far wrong. Again the casualties were concentrated among a few units: the

Maximilien-Sébastien Foy (1775–1825), who proved to be one of Napoleon's most able generals. It was his brigade which made the attack on Piedralonga.

3lme *Léger*, for example, lost some 330 men, and Mermet's casualties included two of his brigade commanders, General Gaulois killed and General Simon Lefebvre wounded. Whereas the British were elated by what they perceived as a victory, Soult's first despatch suggested that he regarded himself as beaten and unable to renew hostilities until reinforced. In that Soult's attempt to prevent the escape of the British had been repelled, the battle could legitimately be regarded as a British victory.

As Hope prepared to embark his troops, a melancholy task had to be performed. Moore had been carried back to his quarters in Corunna by his tearful bearers, and lingered until 8.00pm. He made no complaint, asked after the fate of his aides and friends, and when assured that the French were beaten, said, 'I hope the people of England will be satisfied. I hope my country will do me justice.' He was buried early in the morning of 17 January in the landward bastion of Corunna, next to Robert Anstruther, in a grave dug by men of the 9th Foot, without a coffin, but wrapped in his cloak and a blanket. Charles Wolfe's immortal poem was incorrect in that Moore was not buried 'darkly at dead of night' but the sentiments reflected the army's sense of loss:

> Few and short were the prayers we said,
> And we spoke not a word of sorrow;
> But we steadfastly gazed on the face of the dead,
> And we bitterly thought of the morrow.

At about 9.00pm on the 16th the British troops had begun to withdraw from the positions they had held at the end of the fighting, leaving picquets and camp-fires to conceal their departure. Embarkation continued throughout the night, the picquets falling back under cover of Hill's Brigade at daylight; filthy and ragged from the retreat, and now bloody from battle, the appearance of the troops caused the inhabitants of Corunna to cross themselves as they passed. The guns used in the battle could not be got away, so they were spiked and buried.

When the French discovered that the British had retired, they pushed forward some units towards the Heights of Santa Margarita, firing a few shots about 8.00am just as Rev. Henry Symons, chaplain to the Guards, was conducting the burial service over Moore. By about noon the French had established six guns overlooking the southern end of Corunna Bay and fired some shots at the ships. This caused some consternation: the masters of some transport ships panicked, several ran aground and two were burned, but the effect was minimal, prompting one of Soult's ADCs to compare it to hares squirting water upon the frogs in La Fontaine's fable. The last rearguard, Beresford's Brigade, embarked on 18 January, the Spanish garrison of Corunna under General Alcedo waiting until the fleet was at sea before surrendering to the French.

In four or five days the fleet carried home about 26,000 men of Moore's army, with only slight loss from the wrecking of the transports *Dispatch* and *Smallbridge*, which cost the 7th Hussars some 56 men, the Royal Artillery 22 and the King's German Legion 214 men, seven women and nine children. The troops disembarked in Britain were an appalling sight; James Hale of the 9th remarked that they were so ragged and verminous that they were not fit to march through a clean, Christian country, and most simply burned all their clothing and equipment. So dreadful did Harry Smith appear – 'literally covered and almost eaten up with vermin, most of us suffering from ague and dysentery, every man a living still active skeleton' – that on first seeing him, his colonel exclaimed, 'Who the devil's ghost are you?'[59] The general public reaction, however, may have been that recorded by Christian Heise who overheard a spectator complain that the 3rd Hussars of the KGL had returned without horses or baggage; 'Damn all the horses,' said another, 'Yorkshire has horses enough to mount them again – thank God that the lives of brave men are saved.'[60]

Royal Navy Ships involved in the evacuation:
Ville de Paris (110 guns), *Victory* (100), *Barfleur* (98), *Tonnant* (80), *Zealous* (74), *Implacable* (74), *Elizabeth* (74), *Norge* (74), *Plantagenet* (74), *Resolution* (74), *Audacious* (74), *Endymion* (50), *Mediator* (36), *Cossack* (22), *Gleaner* (ketch), plus transports.

The Royal Navy ships *Alfred* (74) and *Hindostan* (50), and transports, remained at Vigo to embark Robert Craufurd's and Alten's Brigades.

---

55 Hall, p.230
56 ibid., pp.227–28
57 Anon., *Forty-Second*, p.85
58 *United Service Magazine* 1843, Vol.II p.274
59 Smith, p.17
60 Beamish, Vol.I p.185

THE AFTERMATH

Moore's hope that his country would do him justice was echoed by Hope's Corunna despatch, which compared him to James Wolfe in that he was killed too young in the moment of victory, but like Wolfe, 'his memory will ever remain sacred in that country which he sincerely loved, and which he had so faithfully served'. Despite public regret at Moore's death, in some quarters he was severely criticised, even vilified, for what seemed a great reverse – an evacuation with the loss of some 6,000 men. It is still possible to debate the various aspects of the campaign, from its whole concept to the minutiae of Moore's direction of it, but much of the contemporary criticism was influenced by political considerations: as a Whig it was convenient for some to blame Moore rather than the ministry, and this coloured much of the early history. Some of the army joined in the censure, like Alexander Gordon of the 15th Hussars, who claimed that 'the distresses the army encountered are chiefly to be attributed to the misconduct of its leader', whose death at a moment of triumph concealed his errors, 'the ill-judged precipitancy of the retreat, and the undecided measures of the commander'.[61]

The burial of Moore; though in fact it was carried out in early morning, so presumably the lanterns were unnecessary. (Print after T.H. Nicholson)

Many veterans of Moore's campaign lived into the age of photography; this is General Sir James Shaw Kennedy (1788–1865) who as James Shaw was an officer of the 43rd during the retreat, from the effects of which he never fully recovered. The last survivor of the battle appears to have been Thomas Palmer, a soldier of the 32nd, who died in April 1889.

ABOVE, LEFT The memorial plaques to Moore, on the battlefield. The plaque inscribed in Spanish uses the Spanish name for the action, 'the battle of Elviña'. (Ian Fletcher Battlefield Tours)

BELOW, LEFT Moore's tomb, San Carlos Gardens, Corunna. (Ian Fletcher Battlefield Tours)

Conversely, Moore's supporters claimed that Moore's task was both ill-conceived and unattainable, and that he had overcome all the difficulties possible; William Napier, for example, only began his great history of the Peninsular War to vindicate Moore's reputation. Whatever the later political considerations, however, at the time they did not prevent Castlereagh from giving Moore full support, as indeed did the ministry in general. Aspects of the campaign, and Moore's conduct of it, may still be debated; for example, whether he was right to advance where and when he did, whether the speed of the retreat was unduly fast and contributed markedly to the breakdown of discipline and exhausted the troops more than necessary, and over the original uncertainty of the destination of the withdrawal. Against all these questions a central fact must be considered: that Moore was operating without the benefit of adequate intelligence, so that initially he had little idea of the nature and location of his enemies, and was very uncertain about the true state of Spanish resistance and co-operation.

The same strictures affected Napoleon's conduct of the campaign, though this is perhaps less open to debate. His offensive against the principal Spanish armies and his capture of Madrid was a remarkable success, and only compromised by his lack of intelligence concerning the position of the British. Perhaps he should have sent at least a corps further west, to ascertain exactly where Moore was, rather than to presume him to be retiring on Portugal; but when the threat to his communications became obvious, Napoleon acted with exemplary speed. That he was unable to catch Moore in his trap was a matter of time, over which Napoleon had little control. Criticism might be made of Soult for the speed of his pursuit, but the mountainous roads of Galicia were just as difficult for the French to traverse in mid-winter as for the British, and many French troops dropped out from exhaustion. Although Soult was able to utilise those of Moore's supplies which had been left behind and not destroyed, it was remarked about the Battle of Corunna itself that for all their recent tribulations, the British troops had been rested and many re-equipped with new muskets, whereas Soult's infantry was handicapped by damaged ammunition and battered muskets.

If the British left Moore's grave unmarked – 'We carved not a line, and we raised not a stone/But we left him alone with his glory' according to Charles Wolfe – Soult planned a monument to revere his memory. It was La Romana, however, who had the body moved to a more conspicuous position on the south-west of the citadel, over which, in time, an impressive monument was raised. Moore's legacy was more than monuments and a cherished memory, though the consequence of his campaign was more profound than it might have appeared in the immediate aftermath. That consequence can still be debated, but there was much truth in what he reported in his despatch of 13 January to Castlereagh. If his opinion that the Spanish had 'neither the power, nor the inclination, to make any efforts for themselves' was misguided if understandable on account of his personal experiences, he was certainly correct when describing his march to Sahagun: 'as a diversion it succeeded: I brought the whole disposable force of the French against this army'. As William Napier observed, Moore had 'found the means to arrest the course of the conqueror, and to draw him, with the flower of his army, to this remote and unimportant part of the Peninsula, at the moment when Portugal, and the fairest provinces of Spain, were prostrate beneath the strength of his hand',[62] and that Moore had thus intercepted the blow which could have crushed Spanish resistance, and by moving on to capture Lisbon, as had been Napoleon's intention, would have denied to Britain the base essential for the subsequent prosecution of the war. As Wellington himself once suggested, without Moore it is possible that Napoleon could have won the Peninsular War.

61 Gordon, pp.209-10
62 W. Napier, Vol.1 p.464

THE BATTLEFIELD TODAY

As may be seen from some of the modern photographs reproduced in this book (supplied by courtesy of Ian Fletcher Battlefield Tours), some of the terrain over which the campaign was conducted appears substantially unaltered from 1808–09, although changes have occurred to a varying degree: for example, the old Roman bridge over the Esla still exists at Castro Gonzalo, alongside the modern bridge, but little of the castle at Benavente remains. Elsewhere, however, the intervening two centuries have seen much alteration, nowhere more obviously than the battlefield of Corunna itself. Extensive development has pushed out beyond the boundaries of the 'old city' of 1808–09 to cover much of the land that was open at the time of the battle, although some significant locations are preserved. Perhaps the most important is the old church of San Vincente de Elviña, the most famous focal point of the battle (which should not be confused with another Elviña, San Fernando, a short distance to the west). The view from Monte Mero still shows how Soult's position dominated that occupied by the British; Moore would have occupied the former himself had his army been sufficiently strong to hold it. A new bridge crosses the river at El Burgo, next to the remains of the old, and similar relics of the past are visible elsewhere. Modern Corunna shows much concern for its history, and there exists a distinguished local 'Historical and Cultural Association' named 'The Royal Green Jackets', a title also borne by the successor unit of Moore's light troops. A road around San Carlos Gardens, along the walls of the old fortifications, was recently named *Paseo de Sir John Moore* (Sir John Moore Avenue), and in the *Jardin de San Carlos* itself lies Moore's tomb. This impressive sarcophagus, restored in 1824 and 1839 by British subscriptions, is surrounded by the gardens created in his memory in 1834 by the military governor of Corunna, Francisco Mazarredo. Nearby is the military museum. A memorial plaque, installed on the centenary of the battle, marks the location on the *Canton Grande* of the house where Moore died; the original building was demolished in 1977. A further set of plaques commemorating Moore are present on the *Peña de Galiacho*, south of Elviña, on the lower slopes of Peñasquedo, not in the place where Moore received his injury but probably near to the position of the battery which fired the fatal ball. The original plaque bears the simple inscription (in Latin), 'John Moore, general of the British Army' and the dates 16 January 1809 and 19 January 1931, the latter the year in which is was unveiled by the Prince of Wales. The others, in English and Spanish, date from 1997 and also perpetuate Moore's memory and the date and circumstances of his death.

BIBLIOGRAPHY

General histories

Anderson, J.H., *The Spanish Campaign of Sir John Moore*, (London 1905).
Balagny, D.E.P., *Campagne de l'Empereur Napoléon en Espagne*, (Paris 1902–06).
Beamish, L., *History of the King's German Legion*, (London 1832–37).
Cadell, C., *Narrative of the Campaigns of the 28th Regiment since their return from Egypt in 1802*, (London 1835).
Caldwell, G., & Cooper, R., *Rifle Green in the Peninsula*, Vol. I, (Leicester 1998).
Chandler, D.G., *On the Napoleonic Wars: Collected Essays*, (London 1994)
Cope, W. H., *History of the Rifle Brigade*, (London 1877).
Davies, D.W., *Sir John Moore's Peninsular Campaign*, (The Hague 1974).
Fortescue, J.W., *History of the British Army*, Vol. VI, (London 1910).
Hibbert, C., *Corunna*, (London 1961).
Leslie, J.H., *The Services of the Royal Regiment of Artillery in the Peninsular Campaign*, Part II, (London 1908).
Levinge, R.G.A., *Historical Records of the Forty-Third Regiment*, (London 1868).
Londonderry, Marquess of (Charles Stewart), *Narrative of the Peninsular War*, (London 1828).
Moore, J., *Narrative of the Campaigns of the British Army in Spain commanded by Sir John Moore*, (London 1809).
Moorsom, W.S., *Historical Record of the Fifty-Second Regiment*, (London 1860).
Napier, W.F.P., *History of the War in the Peninsula*, Vol. I (2nd edn.), (London 1832).
Napoleon, *The Confidential Correspondence of Napoleon Bonaparte with his Brother Joseph*, (London 1855).
Oman, C.W.C., *History of the Peninsular War*, Vol. I., (Oxford 1902).
Verner, W., *History and Campaigns of the Rifle Brigade*, Vol I (London 1912).
Woolgar, C.M. (ed.), *Wellington Studies I*, Southampton 1996 (includes a chapter by R.J.B. Muir & C.J. Esdaile on 'Strategic Planning in a Time of Small Government', with particular reference to Moore's campaign).

Biographies and memoirs

Anon., *Personal Narrative of a Private Soldier who served in the Forty-Second Highlanders*, (London 1821).
Anon., *A Soldier of the Seventy-First*, ed. C. Hibbert, (London 1975. Originally Edinburgh 1819).
Anglesey, Marquess of, *One-Leg: the Life and Letters of Henry William Paget, First Marquess of Anglesey*, (London 1961).
Blakeney, R., *A Boy in the Peninsular War*, ed. J. Sturgis, (London 1899).
Gonneville, A., *Recollections of Colonel de Gonneville*, ed. C.M. Yonge, (London 1875).
Gordon, A., *A Cavalry Officer in the Corunna Campaign*, ed. H.C. Wylly, (London 1913).
Green, W., *Where Duty Calls Me: the Experiences of William Green of Lutterworth in the Napoleonic Wars*, ed. J. & D. Teague, (West Wickham, 1975).
Hall, B., *Voyages and Travels of Captain Basil Hall RN*, (London 1895).
Harris, B., *The Recollections of Rifleman Harris*, ed. H. Curling, (London 1848, r/p ed. C. Hibbert, London 1970).
Hayman, P., *Soult: Napoleon's Maligned Marshal*, (London 1990).
Ker Porter, R., *Letters from Portugal and Spain*, (London 1809).
Lejeune, Baron, *Memoirs of Baron Lejeune*, trans. & ed. Mrs. A. Bell, (London 1897).
Moore, Sir John, *The Diary of Sir John Moore*, ed. Sir J.F. Maurice, (London 1904).
Moore, J.C., *The Life of Lieutenant-General Sir John Moore*, (London 1834).
Moore Smith, J.C., *The Life of Sir John Colborne, Field-Marshal Lord Seaton*, (London 1903).
Morley, S., *Memoirs of a Serjeant of the 5th Regiment of Foot*, (Ashford 1842).
Napier, G., *Passages in the Early Military Life of General Sir George T. Napier KCB*, ed. W.C.E, Napier, (London 1884).
Napier, W.F.P., *Life and Opinions of General Sir Charles James Napier*, (London 1857).
Neale, A., *The Spanish Campaign of 1808*, (Edinburgh 1826).
Oman, C., *Sir John Moore*, (London 1953).
Parkinson, R., *Moore of Corunna*, (London 1976).
Robertson, O., *The Journal of Sergeant D. Robertson, late 92d Foot*, (Perth 1842).
Ross-Lewin, H., *With the Thirty-Second in the Peninsular and other Campaigns*, ed. J. Wardell, (Dublin 1904).
Schaumann, A.L.F., *On the Road with Wellington*, trans. A.M. Ludovici, (London 1924).
Smith, H., *The Autobiography of Sir Harry Smith*, ed. G.C. Moore Smith, (London 1910).
Steevens, C., *Reminiscences of my Military Life*, ed. N. Steevens, (Winchester 1878).
Surtees, W., *Twenty-Five Years in the Rifle Brigade*, (London 1833).
Tylden, J.M., *The Corunna Campaign 1808–09: Sir J.M. Tylden's Journal*, in *Oxfordshire Light Infantry Chronicle*, (1899).
Verner, W., *Reminiscences of William Verner*, ed. R.W. Verner, (London 1965).

INDEX

COMPANION SERIES FROM OSPREY

MEN-AT-ARMS

An unrivalled source of information on the organisation, uniforms and equipment of the world's fighting men, past and present. The series covers hundreds of subjects spanning 5,000 years of history. Each 48-page book includes concise texts packed with specific information, some 40 photos, maps and diagrams, and eight colour plates of uniformed figures.

ELITE

Detailed information on the uniforms and insignia of the world's most famous military forces. Each 64-page book contains some 50 photographs and diagrams, and 12 pages of full-colour artwork.

NEW VANGUARD

Comprehensive histories of the design, development and operational use of the world's armoured vehicles and artillery. Each 48-page book contains eight pages of full-colour artwork including a detailed cutaway.

WARRIOR

Definitive analysis of the armour, weapons, tactics and motivation of the fighting men of history. Each 64-page book contains cutaways and exploded artwork of the warrior's weapons and armour.

ORDER OF BATTLE

The most detailed information ever published on the units which fought history's great battles. Each 96-page book contains comprehensive organisation diagrams supported by ultra-detailed colour maps. Each title also includes a large fold-out base map.

AIRCRAFT OF THE ACES

Focuses exclusively on the elite pilots of major air campaigns, and includes unique interviews with surviving aces sourced specifically for each volume. Each 96-page volume contains up to 40 specially commissioned artworks, unit listings, new scale plans and the best archival photography available.

COMBAT AIRCRAFT

Technical information from the world's leading aviation writers on the aircraft types flown. Each 96-page volume contains up to 40 specially commissioned artworks, unit listings, new scale plans and the best archival photography available.